# How I play Bridge in Teams

## by

## Professor Bev Pardoe

## About the Author

**Bev Pardoe**
or
**Professor B H Pardoe BSc MSc PhD CEng FIET**

is a retired Professor of Engineering and former Dean of Engineering at the University of Salford, England.
His major interest is steam locomotives with past hobbies of flying aeroplanes and maintaining classic cars. Since 2000 he has played Bridge and this book endeavours to pass on his experience, particularly to "newcomers" perhaps with a scientific bent.

### Acknowledgements
The author thanks his brother, Dudley, for diligently reading the text and making both useful suggestions and detailed corrections.

Published in Great Britain 2023
Pardoe Books, 14 Didsbury Park, Manchester M20 5LJ
© B. H. Pardoe 2023

# Table of Contents

Chapter 1 Introduction ..................................................................... 7
Chapter 2 Foundation ..................................................................... 12
  2.1 Quantification ......................................................................... 12
  2.2 Opening call ........................................................................... 13
    2.2.1 Majority of Hands .......................................................... 13
    2.2.2 Hands with extreme shape ............................................. 14
  2.3 Opening Bids .......................................................................... 14
    2.3.1 Long suits ........................................................................ 14
    2.3.2 Unbalanced Hands ......................................................... 15
    2.3.3 Balanced Hands .............................................................. 17
  2.4 Auctions with out interference, First Response ................... 18
  2.5 Auctions without interference, Opener's second bid ........... 19
    2.5.1 Balanced Hand ................................................................ 19
    2.5.2 Unbalanced Hand ........................................................... 20
  2.6 Auctions without interference, Responder's second bid ..... 22
  2.7 Slam bidding .......................................................................... 22
  2.8 Response to strong 2 openings .............................................. 25
  2.9 The contested auction ........................................................... 27
Chapter 3 Overcalls, Doubles & Defensive Bids ......................... 30
  3.1 The Acol definition of Overcalls ........................................... 30
  3.2 My definition of overcalls ..................................................... 30
  3.3 Doubles for Take-out ............................................................. 31
  3.4 Unusual 2NT ......................................................................... 33
  3.5 Michaels Cue Bid .................................................................. 33
  3.6 Finale ..................................................................................... 34
Chapter 4 Stayman, Transfers & the contested 1NT .................... 35
  4.1 Stayman ................................................................................. 35
    4.1.1 Opener's first reply ......................................................... 35
    4.1.2 Responder's second bid ................................................. 35
    4.1.3 Weak take out in a minor ............................................... 36
  4.2 Transfers ................................................................................ 37
    4.2.1 Responder's First bid ..................................................... 37
    4.2.2 Responder's Second Bid ................................................ 37
  4.3 Responder's response to 1NT ................................................ 38

4.4 The combination of Transfers and Stayman. ...................39
4.5 1NT becomes a contested auction ...............................40
    4.5.1 Bids after RHO bids a suit.* ..............................40
    4.5.2 Wriggle after 1NT doubled* ............................41
4.6 Stayman and Transfer in Tabular form.* ......................42
Chapter 5 Sacrifices and Doubling for Penalties ...................43
5.1 Scoring in Duplicate and Teams. ...............................43
    5.1.1 Scoring in Duplicate. .......................................43
    5.1.2 Scoring in Teams. ...........................................44
5.2 Sacrifices ............................................................45
    5.2.1 Overcalls and Sacrifices. ..................................46
    5.2.2 Pressure and Sacrifices ....................................46
5.3 Negative Doubles .................................................48
5.4 Doubles for Penalties ............................................48
Chapter 6 Defences in Bidding .......................................50
6.1 Introduction ........................................................50
6.2 Defence against weak 1NT ....................................50
    6.2.1 Astro Defence after 1NT opening. .....................50
    6.2.2 Suit Overcalls. ...............................................51
    6.2.3 Doubles and Defences ....................................52
6.3 Defence against weak 2's .......................................52
    6.3.1 Standard 2 Level overcall available ...................53
    6.3.2 Showing a 5:4 hand. .......................................53
6.4 Defence against Multi 2 Diamond ...........................56
6.5 Defence against Doubles and Michael's Cue Bid .......56
6.6 Defence against Weak 3 or more Opening Bids .........57
    6.6.1 2nd Seat: ......................................................57
    6.6.2 4th Seat. .......................................................58
Chapter 7 Must Knows, before playing a hand. ...................59
7.1 The Auction ........................................................59
7.2 The split of the cards* ...........................................59
7.3 A complex auction* ..............................................61
7.4 Keeping track of the cards .....................................62
7.5 Finesse or Drop ...................................................62
7.6 The Knowledge you need ......................................64
Chapter 8 Playing as Declarer ........................................65

4

8.1 Declarer playing in No Trumps....................................................................66
   8.1.1 What do you learn from the lead ..............................................66
   8.1.2 Splits and Card counting* ..........................................................67
   8.1.3 Check their system. ...................................................................72
   8.1.4 Count your winners and note your Controls .............................72
   8.1.5 Techniques during play .............................................................77
   8.1.6 Finessing and Ducking ..............................................................79
   8.1.7 Establishing a long suit..............................................................83
   8.1.8 Using the Auction......................................................................85
   8.1.9 Unblocking during play.............................................................86
8.2 Declarer play in a suit. ................................................................................87
   8.2.1 Short side ruff. ...........................................................................87
   8.2.2 The Cross Ruff ..........................................................................88
   8.2.3 Throw a loser on a winner or a loser. .......................................90
   8.2.4 Finessing in a suit contract .......................................................92
   8.2.5 Establishing a long suit..............................................................93
8.3 Teams versus Duplicate .............................................................................95
   8.3.1 Scoring in Duplicate and Teams ...............................................95
   8.3.2 Examples of play in Duplicate and Teams. ..............................97
8.4 Plays for the expert.*..................................................................................98
   8.4.1 Squeeze plays ............................................................................98
   8.4.2 Strip and Throw-In ..................................................................100
   8.4.3 The Bath Coup as Declarer and Defender...............................102
Chapter 9 Playing as Defenders.........................................................................104
9.1 Discards and Signalling............................................................................105
   9.1.1 Conventions.............................................................................105
   9.1.1.1 Count signals ........................................................................105
   9.1.1.2 Suit signals in suit contracts .................................................105
   9.1.1.3 Suit signals in NT contracts: .................................................106
   9.1.1.4 Discard signals are McKinney, ............................................106
   9.1.2 Double as a signal...................................................................106
9.2 Rule of 11 .................................................................................................107
9.3 Leading through Strength.........................................................................108
9.4 The play as a defender against NT...........................................................109
   9.4.1 The choice of suit to lead. .......................................................109
   9.4.2 Establishing the Defenders Longest suit. ................................115

9.4.3 Managing your long suit, avoid Blocking ............................ 116
9.4.4 Avoiding their suits .................................................... 117
9.5 Playing as a defender against a suit contract ............................ 119
9.5.1 Leads and Signals ..................................................... 119
9.5.2 Forcing Defence ....................................................... 120
9.5.3 Long Suits in a suit contract ......................................... 122
9.5.4 Detecting a Cross Ruff ................................................ 123
9.5.5 Long suit in Dummy and 1 entry ........................................ 124
9.5.6 Finessing Declarer .................................................... 124
9.5.7 Ruff and Discard. ..................................................... 126
9.6 Things not to do as a Defender ........................................... 127
Appendix A .................................................................. 128
THE BASICS .................................................................. 128
Appendix B .................................................................. 130
References and Bibliography ................................................. 130
Appendix C .................................................................. 131
Table 1 4441 ............................................................... 131
Table 2 Responses to 1NT ................................................... 133
Table 3 Transfers .......................................................... 134
Table 4 Stayman after 1NT opening and 2♣ response .......................... 135
Table 5 Stayman & Transfers over suit interference. ........................ 136
Table 6 Wriggle: Transfer over 1NT doubled, for all cases. ................. 136
Table 7 Wriggle For sequence 1NT P P X P P .. ............................. 137
Appendix D .................................................................. 138
Wigan ¾ Howell Movement Cards 4 Tables .................................... 138
Appendix E .................................................................. 139
Bidding (System) Card ...................................................... 139
Appendix F .................................................................. 143
Glossary of Bridge terms ................................................... 143

## * The reader may chose to ignore these sections

# Chapter 1 Introduction

Oh no! Not another book on Bridge. Bridge is a game that is easy to play badly and very hard to play well and everyone who plays it has an opinion on how to bid and how to play the game. Most books are written by successful, usually international, players whereas I have no such pretensions. Having taken up Bridge after retirement, at best I am an average player and write from that perspective. There are various aspects that are under taught or ignored by the experts because often they can play their way out of a hole. The average player wants to be in the right contract based upon all the evidence that can be gained from the auction to maximise their chance of a successful contract and a good score. Note, when I write a masculine pronoun it includes feminine and vice-versa plus any other pronouns you might wish to use.

It is assumed the reader knows the basics of Bridge using the Acol Weak 1 No Trump bidding system and has played some Duplicate Bridge in a Bridge Club environment and wishes to move on. A summary of the basics of that bidding system is given in Appendix A which is a slightly modified version of one given by **Klinger**, Appendix B {1}. All further references in the text will be via a number in {} brackets and can be found in Appendix B by clicking on the link. If you are unclear about several of the items in The Basics, you might like to read a beginners book on Bridge such as {4} before reading this or just come along for an exciting read. An entertaining book {6} and the series by Erwin Brecher and others gives a mixture of conundrums and Bridge hands to solve, I found the problems more interesting than the bridge hands. Some Newcomers will have a greater knowledge about bidding than the information laid out in Appendix A, it is there to define a base line to start from not as a universal claim that this is the knowledge held by all Newcomers. There are items in The Basics that I shall effectively delete or minimise because they are superseded by more detailed consideration of bidding. Examples are semi-balanced hands and minimising the concept of **Forcing**. The foundations of bidding are covered in Chapter 2. Some aspects of bidding are subjected to fashion and dogma so must be treated with care; I shall describe what I have found most productive and predictable.

An area of bidding that is worth considering separately is the area of overcalls, take-out doubles and defensive bidding. This aspect is considered in Chapter 3.

Bridge is a team game, a team of two people who must "speak" the same language and have an agreement on how to approach and play the game. Misunderstandings can be damaging in Duplicate and catastrophic when playing Teams ( a game for at least 4 people on each side) as we shall see later. Teams is my favourite game followed by Pairs and I simply do not play Rubber which I regard as a gambler's game.

I am a fan of counting points and coming to a conclusion based upon the combined strength of the two hands. This is the foundation of Acol that allows you to accurately predict the likely outcome. Acol uses Limit Bids, Wide Ranging Bids and Sign Off Bids to reach the final contract. I extend this concept to **quantification** by describing your hand in the bidding and using preset **boundaries** , covered a little later, to arrive at the final contract. This combination removes much of the need to describe bids as forcing and replacing them with the concept of **"you must bid to the limit set by the bidding so far."** A classic example of this is:

1♠ P 2♠ P 3♠ P 4♠ P P P

1♠ shows 12+ points, 2♠ shows 6 to 9 points, 3♠ shows 16-18 points and 4♠ shows 9 points. More on this in the next chapter.

I rarely use the popular Losing Trick Count, LTC, method making an exception on very distributional hands again more on this later.

The weak 1NT opening is a pre-emptive bid that also pre-empts your partner so we need a system to help each other. Here we use Stayman and Transfers and these are covered in detail in Chapter 4.

An aspect of the game that is rarely taught but essential to get right is the sacrifice. Playing at Teams it is essential to be able to gauge the likely score on a hand for both pairs at the table. This requires two things, a knowledge of the scoring for making a contract or going off doubled and redoubled and the number of tricks likely to be made by both sides. The key to this is an exact estimate of the tricks both sides are likely to make. This can only be done if you bidding system is precise. Here we enter the world of Bashers and Scientist, I am without doubt a Scientist at Bridge as well a Professional Engineer in real life. With my competition partner, the late Colin Skelton, we honed a system of quantified overcalls to enable us to make the right call on sacrifices. Overcalls and take-out doubles are covered in Chapter 3 whilst Sacrificing and doubles for penalties are covered in Chapter 5.

Currently pre-emptive bidding is in fashion with three weak two opening bids being taught by the professional gurus. It is therefore essential to have a well thought out defence strategy to deal with weak 2's and weak 1NT opening bids. One also needs mechanisms to deal with pressurising overcalls such as Michaels Cue bids and the Unusual 2NT. My ideas and implementation are laid out in Chapter 6.

Card play is the most difficult part of the game and the most under taught; possibly because it is the hardest to quantify. I recommend the reader to work through {5} however it does try to be all things to all people so one needs to distil what is important to you and your partner. It gives good backing to the standard leads found on a system cards (see Appendix F). The best book I have found on card play is {8}, you should ignore his quirk about time, whilst the best structured is {16} and {17} is useful.

We can split card play into distinct parts: declarer play and defence play and sub-divide each into suit and NT contracts. Defence being the more difficult and once again it must be emphasised it is a team game whilst declarer play is the one aspect where you are on your own. So a chapter is devoted to each.

There are aspects and foundations to good card play that are common to all forms of play but rather neglected by the references above. These are laid out in Chapter 7 and should be understood before reading Chapter 8 on Declarer play and Chapter 9 on Defender play.

This monograph, hardly a book, is intended to be a dip in and dip out text so each chapter attempts to be stand alone. Also, it does not contain endless examples of hands saying this hand should bid or played like this or that. There is a attempt to generalise the approach into a form that you can use to make decisions at the table rather than learn by osmosis from seeing endless examples. There are $53 \times 10^{27}$ possible different deals, a number so large it is hard to describe without scientific notation so we must create an approach that reduces this number into groups we can deal with, pun intended. This approach tries to break down the decisions into groups and sub groups that ordinary players, like myself, can cope with. I have included a bibliography in Appendix B, these are all books I have used and feel comfortable with. It is up to the reader to use or ignore these books as they see fit or find others that suit them. Today we also have the Internet {18} where there is a lot of information and disinformation, using it with care can be a real bonus. A word from the not so wise, people who write regularly about Bridge in papers or magazines have to find something different to say each day, week or month to justify their pay so beware; they often pick very unusual hands and use an undefined bidding system to come up with a brilliant solution. In reality, an experienced pair, with a well defined bidding system will often bid the right contact, play it flawlessly, but still go off off because no system has been devised (or can be devised?) that covers 100% of those combinations of mega billions of deals that exist. An example is 1NT Pass 3NT followed by three passes. With a good defence this only makes 67% of the time, so what we are aiming for is a system that works most of the time and when it does not, is not a time to try to change one's bidding system or play, to cope with a specific hand.

There is a language of Bridge, English terms and acronyms commonly used that have specific meaning in the context of the game. I shall introduce and high light such terms and have provided a Glossary of Terms and Acronyms in Appendix F, at the end of the book.

Newcomers are often nervous about making mistakes or breaking the the law. My advice is don't worry, we can all get it wrong from time to time and there is a referee, called the **Director** , to sort it out. The most common errors are call out of turn, lead out of turn, insufficient bid and revoke. The latter is not following suit on a trick when you still have a card in the suit. I use the word error purposefully because it very rare to witness someone cheating at Bridge so having the Director called is not a black mark but an opportunity to correct an error and for everyone at the table to learn something about the Laws of Bridge.

This text tries to provide Newcomers with enough insight to feel they have done the right thing and most of the time contracts will make and sometimes you have the joy of making one more trick than anyone else. When games go wrong, they can feel confident that many others will endure the same fete.

**Enjoy your Bridge!**

[Contents](Contents)

## Chapter 2 Foundation

### 2.1 Quantification

Lets start with: you are dealt a hand of cards, now what. Count the cards face down to ensure you have thirteen then view the cards and arrange them into suits in alternating colours. Some people arrange each suit in ascending order whilst others arrange them in descending order; suit yourself there is no right or wrong with this one. Count the number of cards in each suit and check that the sum comes to 13; this avoids one card stuck behind another. Now you have the distribution or shape of the hand, an important attribute. Add up the number of high card points, **HCPs** and add the number of length points,**L** , one for each card more than four in a suit to give your total number of **points**. My first example:

> 89♣ TJ♦ 234K♥ 567KA♠

The shape is [2245] and the strength is 12 **points,** 11 **HCPs** plus 1 **L** point, these are the two crucial attributes of you hand . To be consistent shape in square brackets will always be in increasing rank order of suits but without brackets will be the shape in any order such as 4432 is a balanced hand with no reference to suits. There is the commonly used Rule of Twenty to define an opening bid but it is unnecessary if you use HCPs and length points; using 10 HCPs as a minimum, you can open with 12 points. Length points are used before there is suit agreement and replaced by shortage points when there is suit agreement. Once you have suit agreement you should drop the length points and add shortage points,**S**. For competitive bidding use

**5 for a void, 3 for a singleton and 1 for a doubleton.**

Whenever you reach a suit agreement you must reassess your hand. In the example above you open 1♠ and your partner responds 2♠ so you have a suit fit and reassess your hand. 11 HCPs plus 2 shortage points, S, makes 13 **points**. Throughout the text I shall try to be consistent and use the term **points** for HCPs plus L or S but not booth.

Points=HCPs + L or
Points = HCPs +S with a suit fit.

In some cases length points are kept for an NT call, this may lead to a 3NT call based upon a long minor but less than 25 HCPs. Quantification is the foundation of Acol and leads to the concept of Limit Bids and Wide Ranging Bids. I am amused by people who ask, "do you do quantified bidding?" They are of course asking about a scheme to check for small and grand slams and I am tempted to answer, "yes all the time." Now you have a measure of the hand, the next step is to decide what your opening call will be.

## 2.2 Opening call

### 2.2.1 Majority of Hands

You are the "dealer" and now it is time to look at your hand with the quantification in your mind. We have to divide up those billions of possible hands into manageable groups and I start with shape: do I have 7 or more cards in one suit, do I have six cards in one suit, is my hand unbalanced and finally is my hand balanced. This is almost in reverse order of likelihood. It is worth reiterating something you should know: balanced is one of the following shapes 4333, 4432, 5332 and unbalanced is anything else. I have purposefully excluded the term semi-balanced. You should also note that hands with 6 or more cards in one suit are also unbalanced but have been given a separate category, long suit, because of the the way they will be bid.

A word about fashion and biding systems. I was happy to play Acol, weak 1NT and Acol strong 2's. However, the fashion is for pre-emptive bidding and when you need multiple partners you have to fit in with the fashion, so my preference is now for Benji-Acol which has weak 2's in the majors and 2♣ and 2♦s are strong bids, more on these later. I regard the weak 2♦ as insufficiently pre-emptive and emphasises a minor in a game where all the emphasis is on majors because of the scoring system. There is also a Multi 2♦ opening bid that has merit and would warrant a chapter in its own right but as this text is aimed at Newcomers, I would only advise bidding fanatics to read up about this bid. I shall ignore the weak 2♦ and Multi 2♦ bids until we get to defences against other people's bidding.

### 2.2.2 Hands with extreme shape.

Hands with extreme shapes can be difficult to quantify and here I turn to a system I don't like and only use as a secondary system to quantify my hand: the **Losing Trick Count**, LTC. Part of the system is to count one loser for each missing A, K or Q in each suit but no more losers than you have cards in the suit, e.g. Ax♠ is one loser and xxxx♠ is three losers. A more complete definition and explanation is given in {2}. I have no faith in the system because I have often heard opponents say, when they have missed out on a game contract, "I didn't bid game because the Losing Trick Count gave us only nine tricks." When one reviews the hand after the match, the quantification clearly indicates a four level contract, more on this later. If I pick up a very shapely hand and it has 5 or less loser I will make an opening bid regardless of the point count. Let 's get back to more normal hands; the vast majority of hands that you will have to deal with.

### 2.3 Opening Bids
#### 2.3.1 Long suits.

**7 card suit.** There are three possibilities, with < 6 HCPs, with 6-9 HCPs and more than 9 HCPs.

    < 6 HCPs pass

    6-9 HCPs count your losers, with 7 and non-vulnerable bid 3 of suit

    6-9 HCPs count your losers, with 6 and vulnerable bid 3 of suit.

    > 9 HCPs open one or more of the suit as you have opening points.

    With any other combination pass.

**8 card suit.** You can treat this as a 7 card suit but you need one less loser and bid one more.

**9+ card suit.** This is the realm of the extreme shape that you are unlikely to encounter. I recommend using LTC and bidding accordingly.

**6 card suit.** There are three possibilities, with < 6 HCPs, with 6-9 HCPs and more than 9 HCPs.

    < 6 HCPs pass

    6-9 HCPs bid 2 of the suit if it is a major otherwise pass.

    > 9 HCPs open one or more of the suit as you have opening points.

    With any other combination pass.

#### 2.3.2 Unbalanced Hands

There are a number of aspects to the choice in front of you. With less than opening points Pass ; but with opening points, as the hand is unbalanced you will have to bid a suit so which suit to choose. You have to decide whether it is a normal, strong or single suit hand. You are also telling your partner you will bid again if they respond so you have to prepare a second bid. This is the division of all those billions of hands where you have the most choices, or the most sub-divisions exist. As a general point I never devalue a hand because it has a singleton honour. Although I am writing this in the order you are most likely to encounter hands you may wish to skip forward and read the section on balanced hands and the return to this section.

**A single suiter.** A hand that is too strong for a pre-empt that has one long suit and no other suit that has four or more cards. With a single suiter you intend to bid it and repeat it if you partner responds. We can subdivide a single suiters into normal and strong. Here I shall introduce a new evaluation technique: **playing tricks.**

**How to count playing tricks:**
a. Count every card after the third as one playing trick.
b. In the top three card of each suit, each A and K count as one trick each.
c. Count every Q as a trick if there is a second honour card in suit.
d. Do not count K or Q singleton or Q doubleton.
e. Count only one trick for KQ doubleton.

**In a single suiter count the number of playing tricks and if it is greater than 7 in a major or greater than 8 in a minor bid 2♣** . Note this says nothing about the point count but most hands will have around 17 HCPs. So there is no clear division between strong and normal. When there are less playing tricks but at least 12 points bid one of the long suit.

Most unbalanced hands with 12 to 15 points are covered by biding, as defined in The Basics, Appendix A: higher rank of two 6:6 or 5:5 hands or the longest suit even when holding 5♦ s and 4♥s . The latter may ruffle feathers but to bid otherwise leads you into lying about a major i.e. making your partner believe you have a 5 card major and a 4 card minor. This problem is also minimised by using the negative double introduced, in competitive bidding, later. As an Opener, I never devalue a hand for say a king singleton as I am trying to tell my partner the strength of my hand and have no idea how valuable the king may be. Remember it is a team game, "tell your partner what you have got." Too many times I hear people say, "I thought I would wait and see what you had because I didn't like my hand." I regard this as selfish bidding and leads to your partner not believing your later bids.

With 16-19 points bid as above but **Reverse** on your next bid. An example of a Reverse is:

1♦  P 1♥  P 2♠ …..........

The opener has the 2♦ and 1♠ bids available but passes over them and bids 2♠ . The opener has shown at least 5:4 in ♦s and ♠s and at least 16 points. A similar bidding sequence is:

1♦  P 1♥  P 3♦ …..

which shows at least 6♦s and 16 points. Note with 6:6 or 5:5 hands and 16-19 points you may decide to emphasise a particular suit and so break the "bid the higher ranking suit rule," ( I mean advice, not rule). For both of these bids you must place a **<u>Stop Card</u>** on the table for 10 secs. Before the bid.

With an unbalanced hand and 20-22 points we have a gap in our bidding system.

AKQJx♣  AQJx♦  Kx♥  xx♠

An example of the worst case is given above the shape is 5422 and we have two suits and 21 points, the answer in Benji-Acol is straight forward bid 2♦ where 2♦ is defined as an unbalanced two suiter with at least 20 HCPs or a hand with 23+ HCPs either balanced or unbalanced. It should be noted that using Benji-Acol that a 1 Level opening bid will never contain more than 19 points.

4441 hands. Most people don't like hands with this distribution referring to them as the dreaded 4441 etc. I see them as an opportunity as they contain a singleton and three chance to find a suit fit. When opening the bidding on a hand with only four card suit, bid lowest rank first. There are two cases where you may end up lying but it is only claiming five cards in a minor when you only have four. See <u>Table 1</u> in Appendix C. This is a maxim for all hands that you are opening on that only contain four card suits.

**Bid four card suits up the line.**

### 2.3.3 Balanced Hands.

Now for the **balanced hands**. This is the last sub-division of those billions of hands and contains several of the foundation stones of Acol but your choices are much simpler. 4333, 4432, 5332 are the only balanced hands and I shall exclude two of those immediately. 5332 hands that contain a 5 card major are treated as unbalanced hands because the scoring system favours major contracts, it is important to let your partner know you have a 5 card major even if it is awful, see {3}. Terence Reese says, "bid 1♥ with 2,3,4,5,6 ♥s rather than 1NT." There is a rationale behind this as you are unlikely to establish the heart suit in NTs and make the low rank cards but a trump is a trump. On such hands you bid one of a major and rebid it to show a 5 card suit and a 12-15 point hand. All balanced hand bids are supposed to be at least aiming for NTs but you should think about the two hand combination after each bid is made.

With a balanced hand, no five card major, and 12-14 HCPs open 1NT, this is the Acol weak 1NT and is pre-emptive. I have heard many people say "I didn't open because I only had three As." Losing trick counters might managed to rate such a hand as 10 losers! Remember this is a team game, you must tell your partner what you have even though you are also telling your opponents. I always open 1NT with three As and nothing else as I am telling my partner I have at least 12 HCPs and a balanced hand and I am pre-empting my left hand opponent, LHO. When pre-empting, the maxim "the worse the better" is appropriate about your own hand. Some bidders include 4441 hands in the 1NT bid. I regard this as wrong because it is not a balanced hand and it has potential for a suit contract as it has 3 four card suits and a singleton, see unbalanced hands above. Our definition of a 1NT opening can now be made complete: 12-14 HCPs, balanced and does not contain a 5 card major or a singleton.

With 15-19 HCPs and a balanced hand open one of a suit intending to bid NT at the next opportunity. Here stick to the rule of bid 4 card suits up the line.

With 20-22 HCPs bid 2NTs. There is a case for including a 4441 hand with a singleton A and hands with a 5 card major in this bid. With so many points in one hand there is a danger that you partner will pass a 1 Level bid with 5 HCPs and other shapely hands with less points if you open low. So the definition of a 2NT opening bid is 20-22 HCPs balanced hand that may contain a singleton or a 5 card major.

### Finally, if you don't have a bid Pass

### 2.4 Auctions with out interference, First Response

Responses to 2♣ and 2♦ opening bids are considered in Section 2.8 below. First let us set some **boundaries** based upon the points held by a pair of hands, remember it is a team (of 2) game:

## Boundaries

| Points | Level |
|---|---|
| 18 to 20 | sufficient for 2 of a suit |
| 21 to 24 | sufficient for 3 of a suit |
| 23 to 24 | sufficient for 2NT |
| 25 to 32 | sufficient for 3NT |
| 25 to 29 | sufficient for 4 in a major |
| 29 | sufficient for 5 in a minor. |
| 30 | Think about a slam |

This very important and is the real **quantification of the game**. Here is that same example:

1♠ (12-19) P 2♠ (6 to 9) P 3♠ (16 -19) P 4♠ (9) P P(16-19) P

Responder always has 4 ♠ s as well as the points shown. Learning the boundaries and understanding their application is the only route to accurate bidding. The process is straight forward, assume you partner opens with minimum points and you have four cards in their suit, so bid at the level indicated by points of the combined hands. Without four card support do not bid your partner's suit, find another bid, often 1NT showing 6-9 HCPs and that you do not have four cards in your partner's suit. Bids always carry information in the form of points, a suit and things you don't have. Bidding a new suit at the one level, you must have 6+ points and at least a four card suit. Bidding a new suit at the 2 level you must have at least four cards and 10 points. There is a special case:

1♠ P 2♥ ...

You must have 5 ♥s to make this bid. You have prevented you partner from bidding 2♣ or 2♦ and almost forced a 2♠ bid. So what do you do if you have a [3343] hand with 10-12 points? Bidding 2NT is awful as you have taken up even more bidding space so I recommend lying about a minor and bid 2♣. Almost all other auctions follow a straight forward path, bearing in mind the Boundaries set above, that are laid out in every beginner's book on Acol; but maybe not as explicitly as here.

Two maxims to take away:

*Never support your partner's opening bid with a 3 card suit.*
*Never bid 2NT over a 1♠ opening.*

### 2.5 Auctions without interference, Opener's second bid.

Here I am going to split opener's hand into two types but reverse the order I used before.

#### 2.5.1 Balanced Hand.

When partner has raised your major suit opening bid, you should follow a simply quantified auction using the **boundaries** above. Otherwise, show your strength on your second bid even with a 5332 hand that contains a five card major. With:

15-16 HCPs bid 1NT over a 1 of a suit response and 2NT over a 2 suit response. The latter raises the question, why not 3NT as you must have points for game. It gives the Responder the opportunity to show a 3 card major in response to an initial bid of 1 of a major. If the Opener only has a 4 card major he can bid 3NT otherwise he bids four of the major.

17-18 HCPs bid 2NT over a 1 of a suit response and 3NT over a 2 suit response.

19 HCPs creates a dilemma. If your partner has bid your weakest suit, simply bid 3NT. Otherwise you may have one very weak suit that decent defenders will find and take the contract off. So bid 2NT, not ideal but if one could write a prescription for every scenario the game would not be worth playing.

It should be noted that fashion has moved away from these accurately quantified, Limit Bids, but I have not seen any good reason for doing so and I even use quantified limit bids for over-calls, more on that later.

### 2.5.2 Unbalanced Hand.

There are two divisions here, one, where your partner has raised your opening bid suit and two, your partner has bid a new suit.

**Asking Bids.** When your partner raises your suit you may have a poor suit that you would like help in. Here you can bid a new suit asking for help or telling you have another suit. I recommend all new suit bids, after suit agreement, should be **asking** because some can only be asking. For example:

1♦ P 2♦ P 2♠ ..

Opener is asking for help in ♠ s with an eye for a NT contract. Responder cannot have a 4 card ♥ or ♠ suit otherwise he would have bid them, responder bids 2NT with a stop in spades and 3♣ or 3♦ without. Another example:

1♠ P 2♠ P 3♥ ...

Opener has a weak ♥ suit but can see enough points for 3♠ s however if partner is short or strong in ♥ s, 4♠ s will make. Responder bids 3♠ without help and 4♠ s with help.

**New suit by Responder.** The second division is when partner bids a new suit over the opener's suit. This again falls into two divisions. When Responder has bid 1 over 1 or 2 over one with the 2 bid being of lower rank than the opening bid. e.g.

> 1♦ P 1♥
> 1♥ P 2♦

If Opener has only one suit, he repeats it at the lowest available level to show at least 5 cards and 12-15 points.

> 1♦ P 1♥ P 2♦ ....

A jump bid will show a six card suit with 16-19 points.

> 1♦ P 1♥ P 3♦ ...

The common alternative is that Opener has a four or five card suit lower ranking than the first bid and bids his second suit. This guarantees at least 5:4 in the suits bid and 12-15 points.

> 1♦ P 1♥ P 2♣ ..

With a stronger hand Opener skips over the first suit and bids the second; this shows at least 5:4 in the suits and 16-18 points. The latter is called a **Reverse**; this is an important technique to show a strong unbalanced hand. Examples:

1♦ P 1♥ P 2♣ ...this shows 5:4 in ♦ and ♣ and 12-15 points and denies having 4 ♥ s

1♦ P 1♥ P 3♣ … this shows 5:4 in ♦ and ♣ and 16-18 points, denies having 4 ♥ s and is a **Reverse.**

Many authors / Bridge players will say " a new suit at the three level is Forcing," i.e. partner must bid again. I do not agree with that statement. The same group of people often have a litany of forcing and non forcing bids. I try minimise the use of that term and keep to "**bid to the limit set by the Boundaries.**" Some bids as we shall see are glaringly forcing so you don't have to remember a list of forcing and non-forcing bids. Going back to the example of a Reverse above, the Responder may pass this bid with 4 ♣ s and 6 HCPs, as only he knows there are no more than 24 points in the pair of hands: not enough for game. If the Opener has 19 points, he needs to bid a speculative game or jump Reverse.

## 2.6 Auctions without interference, Responder's second bid.

By this stage as Responder should have enough information to make a final decision. You will know the main shape of both hands and the likely total points in the pair of hands. Clearly, the number of possible combinations is enormous but you should be able to decide the final level of the contract, using the **Boundaries** above and which suit or NT to be in from the bidding. Very often the Responder, with the weaker hand, makes the final decision on the contract by bidding game or passing. There are plenty of players, with the stronger hand, who find this hard to take but it shows a lack of understanding of **Boundaries** and the fact that it is a **team game**. People bring their characters and hang-ups to the game so it is also all about people and personalities, knowing your partner is very important.

### 2.7 Slam bidding

Slam bidding is important but you get very little practice as slam hands occur about once every 24 boards and that is once every two weeks for a pair playing regularly.

There are some simple, rather limited rules dished up in basic Acol bridge:
You need 33-36 HCPs for a Small Slam and 37-40 for a Grand Slam. Coupled to this, for NT slams, is the so called "quantitative" bidding e.g.:
1NT P 4NT bid 6NT if you are maximum otherwise pass.
1NT P 5NT bid 7NT if you are maximum otherwise bid 6NT.
Clearly you can work back from this that the 4NT bidder must have 19-22 HCPs and the 5NT bidder must have 23-26 HCPs.

The Blackwood convention is used to ask for aces and kings when a suit slam is possible.

These are all too limited so I shall introduce three methods with simplifications to make them useful to the Newcomer. After specifying them, I shall return to when to use them.

**Gerber:** after a NT bid, 4♣ s asks for aces **regardless** of the preceding auction. Responses are 4♦ 0/4 Aces, 4♥ 1 Ace, 4♠ 2 Aces and 4NT 3 Aces. If the Gerber bidder finds you have all the Aces he can bid 5♣ asking for Kings. With all the aces and kings 7NT is likely to make.
An example:

1♣ P 1♦ P 1NT P 4♣ (Gerber) P 4♠ ( 2 Aces) P 6NT (3 aces, 33 points)

**Roman Key Card Blackwood, RKCB:** 4NT after a suit asks for key-cards (four aces plus the king of last suit mentioned or the agreed suit) Responses 5♣ 0/3, 5♦ 1 or 4, 5♥ 2 without the Queen of trumps, 5♠ 2 with the Queen. With 5 key-cards and the Queen, 4NT bidder can bid 5NT asking about the three kings, responses 6♣ 0, 6♦ 1, 6♥ 2, 6♠ 3. There cannot be more than 3. Re-bid of the original suit at any stage by the 4NT bidder is a sign-off. An example:

> 1♦  P 2♥  P 4NT(RKCB) P 5♠ (2KCs &Q♥ ) P 6♥   ( 4KCS plus Q)

Note K♥ is a key card, the last bid suit, and 5♠ s is not about spades but says I have 2 key cards and the Q of trumps, in this case ♥s.

**Cue Bidding:** This is useful after a minor suit agreement and for hands with voids. A new suit at the 4 level after suit agreement is a cue bid and is his lowest ace or void which indicates an absolute control. (As ever there is a more complex approach given in {15}.) This process continues until someone decides the final contact. A return to the agreed suit is a sign off and it is assumed one of you has the ace of trumps. One may also bid 4NT, RKCB provided it is safe to do so.

Let's consider the difficult **Cue Bid** first.

> 1♦ P 3♦ ...

Opener reassesses her hand and finds the partnership has at least 32 points. Now 5♦s should be guaranteed but what about 6♦s. The responder may have few high card points plus a void and I shall assume the Opener has 17 HCPs and a void. To bid 4NT would tell you about aces but not which ones and might force you into a 6♦ contract that is not on so a Cue Bid is better. Opener bids 4♥s showing a control in ♥s and implying a control in ♦s as she is interested in a slam but no first round control in ♣s. A new suit at the four level may have the duel purpose of a Cue bid and a suit bid at the same time. Partner bids 4♠s showing a first round control (A♠s or void). Now Opener has a number of possibilities: with second round control in ♣ s bid 6♦s, but without 5♦s. With a void in ♠ s, both hands have first round control in ♠s but no information on ♣s, bid 5♦s. If there is a reversion to RKCB, the trump suit is the original suit agreed not the last suit bid.

Now for **RKCB**:

> 1♣ P 1♠ P 2♠ P 4NT ....

The responder's hand is strong and it contains 18 HCPs and two doubletons so 5♠ s is almost certain and 6♠ s may be possible, note there are at least 32 points ( opener 12-15 points an responder 18 HCPs +2 shortage points) in the combined hands. The Opener may have no key cards and will bid 5♣ s but may also bid up to 5♠ s, 2 key cards plus the Q of ♠ s Responder could pass either and play in 5♠ s. This all works because the suit was ♠ s. Consider

> 1♣ P 3♣ P 4NT ...

Opener is interested in a slam and can't have more than 19 HCPs but may have shortages taking the pair total over 30 points. Any bid above 5♣ s ( 0 key-cards) pushes opener into 6♣ s. The Opener can only bid 4NT if she holds 3 key-cards and the Q♣ as bids of 5♦ or 5♥ force 6♣ s and she will have the required controls. This shows RKCB can be used with a minor but you must be sure that any response is acceptable in the form of pass or bid 6 of the minor. You can cycle through ♦ /♥ & ♠ to check the requirements for RKCB to be used.

Finally **Gerber**:

> 1♣ P 1♥ P 1NT P 4♣ P ...

It is worth repeating the definition of Gerber: after a NT bid, 4♣s ask for aces **regardless of the preceding auction**. Clearly in this auction 4♣s is Gerber. Opener is taken for 15 HCPs balanced with less than 4 ♥s, so how strong does the the Responder have to be? Consider the responder to have 5♥s including the top four honours and four good clubs if Opener has three aces, the Responder can see 4♣ tricks, 5♥ tricks and and 2 aces so with 1 other king 6 NT should make with only 30 HCPs. This is a case for using the LTC, 1NT (15-16) counts as 6 losers so Responder counts her own losers and subtracts the sum from 24, if this is 12 or more bid 4♣ s and continue to 6NT providing they have all four aces. The latter condition is necessary to prevent being taken off in one suit. There seems no point in using quantitative bidding when Gerber is available. Two balanced hands with 32 HCPs and four aces should be sufficient to bid 6NT.

### 2.8 Response to strong 2 openings.

Now I have covered slam bidding we can return to the two strong opening bids, 2♣s and 2♦s. Here are a repeat of their meanings followed by the responses:

### 2♣ opening and response:
As the 2♣ bid indicates a single suited hand with at least 8 playing tricks in a major or 9 playing tricks in a minor, you will only want to play in that suit or NT so all the Responder wants to know is the suit and how many playing tricks the Opener has. Clearly, 2♣ s is **forcing** as Responder does not know which suit is strong.
2♦ : is the only bid to make and the Opener must tell the Responder his suit and number of playing tricks. e.g.
        2♠ 8 playing tricks in ♠ s
        4♦ 10 playing tricks in ♦ s
        3♥ 9 playing tricks in ♥ s
Now the Responder is in control and has three courses of action, bid game with sufficient tricks, pass with no support or check for a Slam if it is likely. Bidding a new suit is a Cue bid showing first round control and 4NT is RKCB.

### 2♦ opening and response:
Lets consider what the bid says: either 23+, balanced or a strong two suiter at least 5/4 and 20+ HCPs. 20 HCPs is an important boundary and fits within the normal quantification of hands. With 19 you open 1 of a suit and your partner responds with 6 HCPs but passes with 5 because game cannot be on so if you open 1 of a suit with 20 HCPs you could miss a game contract when partner has 5 HCPs. However, 1/4 of 5:4 combinations cause problems with the bidding so I shall return to this below. With 20+ HCP and a 6 card suit that does not have enough playing tricks for a 2♣ opening bid you can be 2♦ and if asked for the other suit simply repeat your only suit. You can show extra strength by using follow

on bids. Clearly, **2♦ is forcing.**
**Responders 1st bid:**
**2♥ :** is the most likely bid to make and it asks the Opener to tell you which hand type he has. Opener responds NT, at the appropriate level to indicate a balanced hand with 23+ HCPs and a suit, his longest, to show a 20+ HCPs and at least a 5:4 hand. Once again the Responder is in charge as he is the only one who knows the combined strength of the two hands. Now as there are two minima required to bid game; versus a two suiter at least 5 points and versus 23+ balanced at least 2 points. The 2♥ response should not be seen as entirely negative as there are many hand combinations that may lead to a slam and only in special circumstances will Responder bid anything other than 2♥ s. The only time to do this is when you have a 6+ card suit and at least 5 HCPs. Bidding after a NT response is straight forward and with systems on, you can use Stayman and Transfers after a 2NT bid by Opener. There are problems when the Opener has a strong two suiter. If the Responder has less than 3 cards in the first suit shown with 5+ HCPs or if the Responders has a very weak hand say less than 3 HCPs and no playing tricks, what does he bid. Consider the case when the Opener has 5♥ s and 4♠s and 20 HCPs and the responder has less than 5 HCPs and less than 3♥ s, you are in trouble. These difficulties are a direct product of deciding to include weak 2♥/♠ s as opening bids. Changing one part of a bidding system has a ripple effect upon the whole system that should not be underestimated.

**2♠ /3♣/ 3♦ or 3♥s:** show at least 6 cards in the suit bid and at least 5 HCPs. This is saying we are looking for game somewhere and Opener can respond in various ways depending upon her hand.

**Responders 2nd bid after a suit bid by Opener:**
Let us return to the problem of 2♦ P 2♥ P 3♥ s and the more general 2♦ P 2/3 suit P.... With a very poor hand the Responder must pass hoping the contract has stopped the opposition bidding and making a part score. With 3 cards in the bid suit, you simply bid at the appropriate level including Pass but remember Opener has at least 20 HCP and 22 points with a fit so you only need 3 HCPs to bid game in a major and 7 HCPs to bid game in a minor. But what if you you don't like the bid suit, we can use a standard

mechanism to ask for the other suit: **bid 1 step**. For example, 2♦ P 2♥  P 2♠ P 2NT ( asking for the other suit) and you need at least 2 HCPs to do this as you are forcing the bidding to at least the 3 Level. This brings into focus a problem when the 5 card suit is of lower rank than the 4 card suit and is the adjacent suit, i.e. 5♦s and 4♥s; 5♣s and 4♦s or 5♥s and 4♠s. On these hands, it is probably better for the Opener to devalue her hand and bid 1 of the 5 card suit as an enquiry about the second suit may propel the auction too high. Here is a summary of the bids so far:

> 2♦  P 2♥  P 2NT (23-24 HCPs balanced) P P P
> 2♦ P 2♥  P 2NT P 3NT (2-9 HCPs balanced) P P P
> 2♦  P 2♥  P 3NT (25+ HCPs balanced)
> 2♦  P 2♥  P 2♠ /3♣ /3♦ P bid one step P bid second suit (you chose)

Returning to the worst case 2♦  P 2♥  P 3♥  P, with a stopper in ♠ s and 5 HCPs it would be wise to bid 3NT. Otherwise bid 3♠ believing your partner does not have 4♠ s and you will have to choose between a minor and 4♥ s but with a very weak hand pass 3♥ s.

With stronger hands the Responder can use the techniques of Cue-bidding, Gerber and RKCB to check the possibility of a Slam.

### 2.9 The contested auction.

There are whole books on this subject, see {12} so I shall restrict this section to one or two devices and some general guidance. The principles that can be applied to many combinations are more important than a plethora of examples that only touches the surface of what can turn up. Here my views are definitely contrary to current fashion. I am delighted when the opposition overcall as they are telling me about their hands. Bound up in this is the concept of bidding four card suit up the line, imagine I have 4♦ s and 4♥ s and opened 1♥ when my LHO holds a good 5 card ♥ suit and 8-15 HCPs. , he will pass hoping we end up in ♥ s or NT with his hearts sitting over mine but unknown to me. Not nice! In conjunction with bidding four card suits up the line I use a device the **Negative Double, -veX**. This is not a Sputnik Double, the Sputnik double was invented in the USA, around 1957, in a Strong 1NT / 5 card majors bidding environment. Consequently, it has oddities when used in Acol nevertheless it is commonly used by Acol bidders. I shall define my usage:

### -veX: I would have bid but for the intervening bid.

No bids have to be changed in order to use this definition.
Some examples:
1♣ 1♥ X suggests I have ♦s, I don't have 4♣ , but do have 6-9 points and no ♥ stop for NT, quite a collection for a simple -ve double.
1♣ 1♠ X I may have ♦s or ♥s with 6-9 points and no stop in ♠s for NT. In general the -veX indicates 6-9 points but you may have more and use it to get a second bid from your partner. A particular case is having 10 points and 4 ♥s.
(Consider 1♦ 1♠ X P 2♥ , without the double the Opener would have made a **Reverse bid** : but not in this case as the Responder is showing ♥s
In a Sputnik Double the sequence 1♣ 1♦ 1♠ shows five spades whereas with a -veX it shows 4♠ s and so the Sequence 1♣ 1♦ X shows 4 spades whereas with a -veX it shows no 4 card major, no stop in ♦ s and 6-9 HCPs.)
    The combination of -ve double and bidding four card suits up the line should enable you to avoid supporting your partner with a 3 card suit when they have shown only 4 in the suit.

**My general approach to the competitive auction is to take note of the overcalls but bid as normally as possible.**

You have to ask the Overcaller what the strength of the bid is as this is undefined in every bidding system and is therefore set by agreement between the partners. If you were intending to bid NT you have to check you have a stopper in the over called suit or find a different bid to describe your hand. Typical bids:
  1♦ 1♠ (8-15) 2♣, the last bid still means at least 4♣ s and 10 points.
  1♦ 2♠ (intermediate) X , I have 10-12 points and no spade stop, <4♦ s.

    Due to shape it is possible for 4♥ to make one way and 4♠ to make the other way. One must consider how much your own auction depends upon shape as this will give you some insight into what the opposition are bidding on.

There will be more on the contested auction after I have covered overcalls and doubles. Contested auctions may also appear in examples on any aspect of bidding. Clearly, we now have to cover Overcalls, Doubles and deal with special overcalls. These are covered in Chapter 3.

Contents

# Chapter 3 Overcalls, Doubles & Defensive Bids

## 3.1 The Acol definition of Overcalls

Basic Acol over-calls are defined as :
1 Level a good 5 card suit with 8-15 HCPs,
2 Level without a jump, a good 5 card suit and 10-15 HCPs, and
Double jump over call weak 7 card suit 6-9 HCPs.

Acol does not define the strength of a jump overcall and you will find three common definitions in use: weak 6 card suit, 6-9 HCPs; intermediate 6 card suit 12-15 HCPs and strong 16+ HCPs. It is important to ask your opponents what they their definition of a jump overcall is.

A useful approach to Conventions and Defensive bids is given by {14}.

## 3.2 My definition of overcalls

Overcalls as used in my Benji-Acol, Weak 1NT bidding system are not standard Acol but have some extra merit.

Overcalls may fulfil four different functions, initially they indicate a possible lead to your partner, with support from the **Advancer** they can turn into a mechanism to pressure the opposition into over bidding their hands, reaching a sacrifice or even a final contract. Some years ago whilst playing Teams, my partner (the late Colin Skelton) and I decided we could not quantify overcall hands accurately and this prevented us from knowing when to stop and when to sacrifice. I cover **Sacrifices** in Section 5.2 . We decided that overcalls should be accurately defined and simplified. We trialled our own definition of overcalls when playing Teams and it worked so well we used it in Duplicate as well.

We came up with a set of overcalls that are better quantified than the Acol definitions, almost Limit Bids. A fundamental shift was to remove the concepts of jump and double jump overcalls as these bids are hard to make and stay within the definition of the boundaries. Our definition of overcalls are:

**1 Level**  good 5 card suit and 8-11 HCPs
**2 Level**  good 6 card suit and 12-15 HCPs. An exception is the 2♣ overcall, as there is no such thing as a 1♣ overcall so this leads to 2♣s being defined as 8-15 HCPs and a good 5 card suit.
**3 Level**  7 card suit and 6-9 HCPs.
With 16+ HCPs just double, X, for take out.
One definition of good is given by {1}: suit quality, SQ (also known as SQOT) is obtained by adding the number of honours to the number cards in the suit and this should be greater than or equal to the number of tricks you have bid to make. An example is KQxxx gives suit quality, SQ = 7 so is a good suit at the 1 Level. KQJxx and AQxxxx both have an SQ of 8 and both may be regarded as a good suit for a 2 Level contract. Making an overcall using these definitions enables the Advancer to support or pass using the Boundaries set in Chapter 2. I shall deal with sacrifices in Section 5.2 A non-sacrifice example:

1♥, P, 2♥, 2♠ P 3♠ P 4♠ ….

1♥ is an opening hand, 2♥ four card suit 6 to 9 HCPs, 2♠ 6 card suit, SQ=8 and 12 to 15 HCPs, 3♠ 2+ card suit 10-12 points, 4♠ 15 points. We have accurately arrived at a game contract where one could raise the question, how does a pack contain 43 points. The answer is straight forward as the combination of HCPs and shortage can readily exceed the 40 HCPs. For example a deal with four voids will give a 60 point pack whilst there are still only 40 HCPs.

1♥ 1♠ 2♥ 2♠ P P 3♥ P P P

This illustrates an attempt to push the opening pair into an un-makable contract. The Advancer is absolutely minimum for his bid and it turns out so is the Overcaller. Although the opening pair were happy to play in 2♥s they have been pressured into playing in 3♥s. This type of auction often happens and both sides turn out to have 20 HCPs.
These two examples are also examples of contested auctions.

### 3.3 Doubles for Take-out.

Listening to people I am frequently amazed at the lack of clarity around take-out doubles. The simplest is generated by a 4441 hand where the singleton is the suit bid by the Opener: but what strength do you need to Double, X. Your hand should become an opening hand, 12 points, with a suit fit and there are three possible suit fits so the odds are good.

We can list the minimum HCPs by hand shape when you are the Opener's LHO or the RHO when the Responder passes:
4441  9 HCPs + 3 for singleton = 12 points,
5440  7 HCPs + 5 for a void = 12 points,
4432  11 HCPs + 1 for doubleton =12 points but you must have a strong 3 card suit because you may end up in a 4:3 fit with your partner. Many people use the last shape but I don't; I would rather defend with this hand. An example of the pitfall of X on a 4432 hand is:

> 1♥ X 2♥ 4♠ P P P …

The Advancer might have 4♠ **rags** and 13 points with distribution. It will be difficult to make as they may well have two heart tricks and two spade tricks taking the contract 1 off.

Another possibility is they have bid two suits and you have four cards in each of the unbid suits. You can make a take-out double so long as you have 12 HCPs. Your partner is then in a position to respond appropriately. For example:

> 1♦ P 1♥ X 2♥ 2♠ ………

Your partner has 4 ♠ s and 6-9 points.

Finally a hand containing 16+ HCPs and not suitable for a 1NT overcall, see later, you can double in either seat for take-out. If your partner responds you have to raise his suit or change suit to show your strength.

> 1♥ X 1♠ 2♣ (6-9 points and 4+♣ s) 2♥
> 2NT ( 16+ HCPs balanced stops in ♥ s and ♠ ) …..

> 1♥ X 1♠ 2♣ 2♥ 3♣ ( 16-18 points and 4 ♣ s) …

With more points, Advancer and Overcaller bid up to a level set by the Boundaries.

A rare example, from me, of forcing, it should be noted that if your LHO passes then your partner is forced to bid.

> 1♥ X P 2♣ P P P …

The Advancer was forced to bid and could have 0 points.

The opposition can fight back against the X by using a **Stretch Raise.** If the Responder has 4 of the Opener's suit, ♥s in this case, he can bid as follows: 2♥s showing 0-5 points, 2NT showing a normal raise to 3, 10-12 points, or 3♥s showing 6-9 points. This makes it difficult for the Advancer to bid naturally. Another example of a contested auction.

### 3.4 Unusual 2NT

You pick up a hand with 2 five card suits and at least 8 HCPs. Why 8 , because with a suit fit you will have at least 12 points, making it an opening hand. Your RHO opens the bidding with 1♥ and you have 5♣s and 5♦s so you bid 2NT. Your partner can assess his hand knowing which suits you have and your minimum strength. This enables him to make a suitable response as Advancer. To be precise, your are saying I have the **two lowest unbid suits**, for example the Opener bids 1♦ and you are 5:5 in ♣s and ♥s so your bid is still 2NT. Clearly, you may end up in a 3 Level contract you can't make but you have cut your opponents out. If the responder passes you are forced to bid.

1♥ 2NT P 3♣ P P P

The Advancer has more ♣s than ♦s.
There is a pattern emerging here:

*if your partner makes a conventional bid that is passed by your opponent you are forced to bid,*

this applies everywhere consequently we don't need a list of forcing bids, just a clear definition when we have to reply.

### 3.5 Michaels Cue Bid

You pick up a hand that is 5:5 in the majors, yes this is the complement of the Unusual 2NT and follows the same definitions and the strict definition of the bid is 5:5 in the **two highest unbid suits** with at least 8 HCPs. The bidding goes 1♥ 2♥ .... and the 2♥ bid is a Michaels Cue bid showing 5:5 in ♠s and ♦s. You might even bid as follows: 1♣ P 1♥ 2♣ .... showing ♠s and ♦s, 5:5 ; this links to a X in the same position showing 4:4 in the unbid suits but a stronger hand. These two conventional overcalls contain the useful attribute that they give your partner a choice of two suits and he only needs 3 card support to assess his hand for points and decide the level of response that is appropriate. The technique of giving your partner two choices will crop up later, several times, in defences against various bids.

Examples of Michaels Cue bids:

> 1♥ 2♥ P 2♠ forced, may have 0 points but more ♠s than ♦s,
> 1♥ 2♥ 3♣ 3♠ will have at least 3 ♠s and 10 points and
> 1♥ 2♥ 3♣ P less than 10 points.

For every measure there is a counter measure see section 6.5 .

## 3.6 Finale

*Again , If you don't have an overcall, X or defensive bid, Pass.*

Contents

# Chapter 4 Stayman, Transfers & the contested 1NT

Most newcomers have been taught Stayman and the minority Transfers. I shall cover both in detail because there is a wide range of possibilities and variation. For those who like tables, see Section 4.6 (this Section and the tables may be ignored on first reading). I shall also assume that Stayman and Transfers are both part of the bidding system.

### 4.1 Stayman

Your partner opens a weak 1NT and you bid 2♣. This is a conventional bid, Stayman and requires the Opener to reply with bids that have a specific meanings. However, there are also limits on your own hand, I shall let these unfold through the bidding examples and summarise them later.

### 4.1.1 Opener's first reply

Your partner opens 1NT and you bid 2♣s and partner announces Stayman but what is the Responder telling his partner? Many players, even very experience players, would say he is showing at least 1 four card major, but this is not true. Also, remember, we have specified that the 1NT opening bid does not contain a 5 card major.
Examples :

> 1NT P 2♣ P 2♦, no four card major
> 1NT P 2♣ P 2♥, 4 ♥s
> 1NT P 2♣ P 2♠, 4♠s

With two four card majors the Opener should bid 2♥ s, More on this later. The 2♣, Stayman bid has required the Opener to bid a four card major or 2♦ s if he does not have a 4 card major. This is the convention but we have still not defined what the Responder's suit or strength is.

### 4.1.2 Responder's second bid

The Responder's second bid will tell the Opener more about his hand. The following are examples of the Responder's possible replies:

> 1NT P 2♣ P 2♦ /♥ /♠ P Pass

2♦ /♥ /♠ is short hand for the Opener has bid 2♦ or 2♥ or 2♠, the only bids Opener is allowed to make, this is followed by a Pass from the Responder which indicates a weak hand, 0-10 HCPs with at least 4 cards in Opener's response.

> 1NT P 2♣ P 2♦ /♥ P 2♠

The responder has 5 ♠s and 4♥s or 4♦s and is weak, 0-10 HCPs. He can pass the Opener's reply or bid 2♠s as a weak take out.

> 1NT P 2♣ P 2♦ /♥/♠ P 2NT

The Responder has 11-12 HCPs and at least 1 four card major but not the one bid. However if the Opener bids, say 2♥s, and the Responder has 4♥s, he will bid 3♥s inviting Opener to bid game if he has maximum points, 14 HCPs.

> 1NT P 2♣ P 2♦ /♥ /♠ P 3NT

The Responder has 13-19 HCPs and a four card major but not the one bid.

> 1NT P 2♣ P 2♥ /♠ P 4♥ /♠ ,

The Responder bids game, has 4 cards in the major bid and 13-19 HCPs.

### 4.1.3 Weak take out in a minor.

As we are using Stayman and transfers, 2♣s and 2♦s are conventional bids and cannot therefore be used for a weak take out. The Stayman bid can also be used for a weak take out in a minor. If the Responder wants to make a weak take out in a minor, he bids 2♣s Stayman and follows it with a 3 level bid in ♣s but may pass 2♦s if that is his weak minor:

> 1NT P 2♣ P 2♠ P 3♣ ... at least 6♣ s but less than 8 HCPs
> 1NT P 2♣ P 2♠ P 3♦ ... at least 6♦ s but less than 8 HCPs
> 1NT P 2♣ P 2♦ P P .... at least 6♦ s but less than 8 HCPs

If the Opener bids 2♦ the Responder can pass as he has achieved his goal. The 3♣ problem is that we have lost the 2♣ weak take out so we must have a route to a weak contract in ♣s. There are two ways to do this either by using a 2♠ bid or including it in Stayman. When invented the Stayman bid included a weak take out in ♣s and ♦s as described above and is sometimes described as non-promissory Stayman, that is not promising a four card major.

### 4.2 Transfers

The Transfer was introduced to extricate you from being pre-empted by your partner when he opens a weak 1NT but of course the transfer has taken on a life of its own. I shall reconcile Stayman and Transfers in section 4.4.

#### 4.2.1 Responder's First bid

Your partner opens 1NT and you have a five card major, your first thought should be transfer no matter what your strength, not quite true but let's define Transfers:

> 1NT P 2♦  P 2♥ ..   ♦   transfer, at least 5 ♥s
> 1NT P 2♥  P 2♠ ...  ♥   transfer, at least 5♠s

The one exception is when you have 13+ HCPs and a five card major; always bid 2♣ Stayman and then bid a Game choice.

> 1NT P 2♣ P 2♦ P 3♥ ...

The 2♣ ; 3♥ combination is telling the Opener, we have game points, please bid 4♥s if you have 3♥s or 3NT with less than 3 ♥s. With less points Responder would transfer to ♥s first then invite game.

The Opener may bid 3 of the major showing 14 HCPs and 4 cards in the implied major. This is referred to as a super accept.

> 1NT P 2♥ P 3♠ ...

Note the Responder bids in accordance with the combined strength of the hands and the <u>Boundaries</u> as she can nominate the Opener with 13 HCPs and add to that her own points.

#### 4.2.2 Responder's Second Bid

The Responder's second bid depends upon her strength and shape:
0-10 HCPs Pass
11-12 HCPs you can invited game.

13-17 HCPs and a six card major, bid game.
With 15+ HCPs and 5 in a major plus 4 in a minor ; after a transfer, bid 3 of the minor, as an indication of strength and a 5:4 hand.

> 1NT P 2♦ P 2♥ P 3♦ ....

The Responder must be at least 5:4 in ♥s and ♦s but must also be strong as with a weak hand there is no point in venturing to the three level and with a game going hand in ♥s or NTs; an invitation would be made, so this has to be a strong hand. The Opener with 2♥s and 3♦s , bids 3NT and the Responder's further bids depend upon the contents of her hand.

### 4.3 Responder's response to 1NT

Having laid out the conventions we can consider the normal flow of the bidding. Your partner has opened a weak 1NT, now you survey your hand. We can recap, the 1NT shows 12-14 HCPs a balanced hand that does not contain a 5 card major. With a balanced hand you will be looking for a NT contract but with an unbalanced you would prefer a suit contract. The latter is particularly true if you have a weak hand with a long suit. You will not have the strength to establish the lower cards in NT nor the power to return to the weak hand so you should be looking for a suit contract. Also, because of the scoring system, finding a major suit fit is more important than a minor suit fit. All of these points leads us to using minor suits after a 1NT bid by the opener to find a major suit fit. The two techniques we have are Stayman, 2♣ s and Transfers, 2♦/♥ .

Now the Responder can view his hand in the light of these two techniques after his partner has bid 1NT. Is Responder's hand unbalanced or balanced:

**Unbalanced** 0-12 HCPs
with 5 or more in a major consider a transfer
with 5 in a minor Pass
with 6 or more in a minor and 0-7 HCPs bid 2♣s
with 6 or more in a minor 8-12 HCPs Pass
**Unbalanced** 13-19 HCPs bid 2♣s
**Unbalanced** 20+ HCPs and a five card suit bid 3 ♣ /♦ /♥ /♠
    It would be nice to have a bid that means tell me your 2 card suit

but we don't and the nearest we come is bidding 2♣ without a four card major and and unbalanced hand. The scope of the Stayman bid has increased again.

**Balanced** 0-10 HCPs pass
**Balanced** 11-19 with a major bid 2♣ s
**Balanced** 11 without a major bid 2♠ s
**Balanced** 12 without a major bid 2NT
**Balanced** 13-19 without a major bid 3NT
**Balanced** 20+ HCPs bid 4♣ s Gerber

The 2♠ and 2NT bids are now conventional bids stating Responder has a balanced hand an an exact number of points. The Opener can bid 2NT or 3NT (with 14 HCPs) after 2♠ and Pass or 3NT (with 13-14 HCPs) after 2NT.

Not every combination of hand is listed here but you should be able to decide upon your first response and successive bids based upon the combination of suits, HCPs and the Boundaries set in Chapter 2.

### 4.4 The combination of Transfers and Stayman.

There are three sections to the response to a weak 1NT opening when we employ Stayman and Transfers. Lets consider it from the bids available rather than Responder's hand shape and strength.

The bids 2♠s to 4♣s have specific meanings with limited variation.

The bids 2♦s and 2♥s are transfers to 2♥s and 2♠s respectively and come with a guarantee of at least a five card suit but no guarantee of any points. The Responder may bid on with a stronger hand.

Finally we have the 2♣ bid which is recognised as Stayman but comes with multiple meanings from the Responder. Responder may have one of the following:

A weak take out in a minor,
A weak 4441 or 5440,
A weak 5:4 in majors,
11-19 HCPs with at least one four card major or
13-19 HCPs, enough for game , with an unbalanced had.
So you thought Stayman was simple, unfortunately it is not but the bids fall into a well regulated pattern.

For those who like tables, this structure of responses is given in Appendix C Table 2, this is followed by Transfers and responses in Table 3 and Stayman and responses in Table 4.

### 4.5 1NT becomes a contested auction

After your partner opens 1NT his RHO will often bid making it difficult for you to make your bid based upon transfers and Stayman. You must make an agreement with your partner to play **systems on** or **systems off**. Systems off means that you abandon transfers and Stayman after interference and make natural bids that describe your hand, I do not recommend this but if you do you can ignore the next two sub sections. Systems on means you try to continue, where possible with Stayman and transfers and in the case of a X we add a little and the system becomes a Wriggle.

#### 4.5.1 Bids after RHO bids a suit.*

Keeping systems on, where possible we try to use Stayman and transfers. Some examples:

> 1NT 2♣ X ….

whatever the 2♣ bid means the X says that was my bid i.e. Stayman.

> 1NT 2♥ X…….

whatever the 2♥ bid means the X says that was my bid i.e. transfer to ♠s.

> 1NT 2♦ 2♥ ….

whatever the 2♦ bid means the 2♥ says transfer to ♠s. Where the 2♦ bid indicates ♠s and another suit, it would be wiser to pass rather than show your ♠s.

Of course there are times when you cannot bid because you hand is not right for a 3 Level bid and you have no 2 Level bid available. Clearly, the higher the RHO bids the more difficult it is for the responder. A summary is given in Appendix C Table 5 Transfer over suit interference.

#### 4.5.2 Wriggle after 1NT doubled*

The RHO has more points than the opener and normally a balanced hand; you want to escape from 1NTX and the race is on to find the best suit fit with the Opener. The Responder wants to show a 5 card suit if he has one but keep the his partner as declarer. The principle of transfer is extended to all suits but there is no suit lower than ♣s to bid as a transfer to ♣s. This is overcome by using the redouble, XX as transfer to ♣s.

Of course, the Responder may not have a five card suit and anywhere from 0 to 13 HCPs; this problem is overcome by making a Pass forcing that indicates that the bidder has no five card suit or has more than 8 HCPs. The Opener is required to XX giving the Responder the option to pass for penalties or bid a 4 card suit up the line. Some examples:

1NT X P^ P XX P 2♥ ….

P^ is a forcing Pass and the XX keeps the bidding going, Responder has 4♥s and 0-8 HCPs

1NT X 2♣ P 2♦ …

Responder has 5♦s and 0 to 8 HCPs

The Advancer may intervene with a suit bid that absolves the Opener from having to transfer or XX. In this case it is usual for the Opener to pass gracefully ( or do I mean gratefully) as he has escaped from 1NTX which was the Responder's main objective. A summary of likely bids is given in <u>Table 6</u> Appendix C.

There is one more problem, when the bidding goes 1NT P P X P P, if the Responder passes the, the auction will be terminated so he can't make a forcing pass. The Responder will not have 5 ♥s or 5♠ as he did not transfer at the first opportunity but may have 5♣s or 5♦s, this creates a dilemma. If we use XX for transfer to ♣ s we have no mechanism to deal with 4 card suits so we drop transfers all together and use XX, with 0-8 HCPs, to ask the Opener to bid again. Bidding 2♣s or 2♦s become a natural 5 card suit bid. With 9-12 HCPs simply pass the X for penalties. Some examples:

1NT P P X P 2♦ …

shows a five card ♦ suit and 0-8 HCPs

1NT P P X P XX P 2♦ ..

show opener's lowest 4/5 card suit and Responder passes unless he has less than 3 cards in the suit:

> 1NT P P X P XX P 2♦ P 2♠ ..

this is the worst case , Responder has 4♣s, 2♦s, 3♥s and 4♠s.
Nearly always the Advancer will bid a five card suit and you drop out of the auction. The bids are summarised in Table 7 Appendix C.

### 4.6 Stayman and Transfer in Tabular form.*

AS mentioned before, I have laid out the possible bids in tabular form in Appendix C Tables 2, 3 and 4.

Table 2 Summarises the meanings of the Responder's first bid after partner bids a weak 1NT. It also includes the Opener's replies to the two Limit bids 2♠ and 2NT

Table 3 gives all the sequences of Responder making a transfer followed by the Opener's reply and the Responder's final bid.

Table 4 Gives the Opener's reply to 2♣ , Stayman and the Responder's second bid. There may be a third bid from both the Opener and the Responder before the contract is finalised.

I have tried to make the bidding as water tight as possible but there may be very rare hands not covered by the tables. It is important to remember a bidding system is a guide not a recipe.

Contents

# Chapter 5 Sacrifices and Doubling for Penalties

Before we can consider sacrifices and doubling for penalties, we must be clear about scoring and the game we are playing.

### 5.1 Scoring in Duplicate and Teams.

It is assumed the reader is familiar with the scoring of a contract based upon the outcome: e.g.
- 4♥ Vulnerable 1 off, 100 points
- 4♠ non-vulnerable making, 420
- 3♦ X non-vulnerable making 11, 670
- 1NT either vulnerability making, 90

The scores are the same whether you are playing Duplicate or Teams however the implications are different.

### 5.1.1 Scoring in Duplicate.

In Duplicate let us consider a match where there are 4 tables and 6 rounds of 4 boards each. Each board is played 4 times and you play 6 rounds against 6 other pairs, you don't play against 1 pair and which one depends upon where you start. As an example, this could be played as a Wigan ¾ Howell movement and the movement cards are given in Appendix D. After playing all 24 boards you get a % score and a rank order based upon your %. Now each pair plays 24 boards and if you made one more trick than everyone else on each board you would gain 100% so each board is worth 4 1/6 %. Dropping the fraction, if you make a mess of the bidding or play on one board you lose 2% relative to the mean. Consequently, the score on one board will not significantly affect your match score. A typical range of scores for 24 boards is 30 to 70 % because a number of boards will always result in the same contract making the same number of tricks and everyone gets 2%. So success is achieved by being in the right contract and making one more trick than anyone else. Defending well in a part score or game contract making one extra trick is just as important as making an extra trick in a small slam.

### 5.1.2 Scoring in Teams.

Scoring in Teams is different. Usually two teams of four play 24 boards. The home team sits NS at one table and EW at another and remain there for the whole match. In the first half, Team A NS plays 12 boards against Team B pair a and at the same time, Team A EW plays the same 12 boards against Team B pair b. After half time refreshments, Team A NS plays against Team B pair b and Team A pair EW plays Team B pair a for a further 12 boards. In this way each pair plays 24 boards and plays 12 against each pair of the opposing team.

Here is an example of scoring in a Team match on the first 4 boards: The first four boards.

| Hand No. | VUL. | Versus TEAM or PAIR No. | CONTRACT | BY | TRICKS | SCORE PLUS | SCORE MINUS | MATCH POINTS A | MATCH POINTS B |
|---|---|---|---|---|---|---|---|---|---|
| 1/ | — | A NS | 4H | N | 10 | 420 |  | 0 |  |
| 2/ | NS | A NS | 6S | N | 12 | 1430 |  | 13 |  |
| 3/ | EW | A NS | 2H | E | 8 |  | 110 | 0 |  |
| 4/ | ALL | A NS | 3H | N | 10 | 170 |  |  | 6 |
| 5/ | NS |  |  |  |  |  |  |  |  |

| Hand No. | VUL. | Versus TEAM or PAIR No. | CONTRACT | BY | TRICKS | SCORE PLUS | SCORE MINUS | MATCH POINTS |
|---|---|---|---|---|---|---|---|---|
| 1/ | — | A EW | 4H | N | 10 |  | 420 |  |
| 2/ | NS | A EW | 4S | N | 12 |  | 680 |  |
| 3/ | EW | A EW | 2S | N | 6 | 100 |  |  |
| 4/ | ALL | A EW | 4H | N | 10 |  | 620 |  |
| 5/ | NS |  |  |  |  |  |  |  |

Match points in IMPS:

```
IMP    0 -   10 = 0 IMP    320 -  360 =  8 IMP    1300 - 1490 = 16 IMP
      20 -   40 = 1 IMP    370 -  420 =  9 IMP    1500 - 1740 = 17 IMP
      50 -   80 = 2 IMP    430 -  490 = 10 IMP    1750 - 1990 = 18 IMP
      90 -  120 = 3 IMP    500 -  590 = 11 IMP    2000 - 2240 = 19 IMP
     130 -  160 = 4 IMP    600 -  740 = 12 IMP    2250 - 2490 = 20 IMP
     170 -  210 = 5 IMP    750 -  890 = 13 IMP    2500 - 2990 = 21 IMP
     220 -  260 = 6 IMP    900 - 1090 = 14 IMP    3000 - 3490 = 22 IMP
     270 -  310 = 7 IMP   1100 - 1290 = 15 IMP    3500 - 3990 = 23 IMP
                                                  4000 and up = 24 IMP
```

The first score card belongs to Team A NS and the second is from Team A

EW, Team B will have mirror images of these two cards, I have chosen the stationary team to illustrate some important points, pun intended. On board 1 the contract was 4♥ s played by North at each table and both made 10 tricks. The net score is found by adding the two cards 420 + (-420) = 0 and the IMP table gives 0 so enter 0 match points for Team A. On board 2, N plays in 6♠ s making 12 tricks whereas at Table 2 N plays in 4♠ s making 12 tricks. This gives a net score of 750 to Team A and the match point table gives 13 IMPs. Following the same process the IMPs for board 3 are 0 and board 4 are -6, i.e 6 for Team B. The overall score is found by adding up the match points on all 24 boards, usually carried out at half time and full time. A typical score would be 56:47 for A:B indicating A won the match by 9 Match Points.

Now we can consider the importance of bidding a slam if it is possible or likely to make rather than settling for game. Equally, not bidding game when it is possible to make a game is a disaster. In the example above Team A bid and made a slam whilst Team B bid game and made 12 tricks. This gave Team A 13 IMPs and was enough to turn defeat to victory. One bad board can lose you the whole match at Teams whilst at Duplicate it might reduce your rank by one place. This leads to the idea of bidding game or a slam on one point less than you would do in Duplicate. Consider the bids at the beginning of this section made at Teams:

3♦ X making 11 670 points versus 3♦ making 11 150 points

This gives a net score of 520 points and results in 11 IMPS to the side that **did not** double. Consider the auction:

1♠ P 3♠ P 4♦ P 4♥ P 6♠ X(P) P P

You hold the A♠s and the AK of ♦s so Double. No! Why not, the bidding shows declarer has first round control of ♦s, as 4♦ s is a Cue bid, you know this must be a void so you are not likely to make either of your ♦ honours. In Teams never double a contract unless you are sure to take it off. That is quite a high bar but doubling a contract into game usually costs you the match.

## 5.2 Sacrifices

### 5.2.1 Overcalls and Sacrifices.

We can now consider sacrifices in both Duplicate and Teams. First sacrifices are more likely to be beneficial when they are vulnerable and you are non-vulnerable so lets consider that case first. An example: dealer is North,

1♠ 2♥ 2♠ 3♥ 4♠ 5♥ P P X P P P

Using typical Acol definitions of overcalls, they do not contain sufficient information to ensure the 5♥ bid is wise or not so I shall use my definition of overcalls given in section 3.2 and repeated here for clarity:
> **1 Level 8-11 HCPs 5 card suit SQ 7**
> **2 Level 12-15 HCPs 6 card suit SQ8**
> **3 Level 6-9 HCPs 7 card suit.**

In the example auction above, the Overcaller has 8 HCPs and the Advancer must have at least 14 points, with 16 he would bid game in Teams but with 17 in Duplicate. After the confidant bid of 4♠s by N, E has to make a decision: let them play in 4♠s and try to take it off or bid 5♥s, perhaps get doubled, and take the loss. E has only 8 HCPs and no features that suggest that he can make more than 9 tricks in ♥s but going two off, doubled, non-vulnerable will only cost 300 points versus NS making 4♠s vulnerable 620 points. Lets assume that 4♠s makes 10 tricks and 5♥s makes nine tricks no matter who plays it. In duplicate you will find NS results: 100, 300, 620. which equate to an EW top, average and NS shared top. The exact percentage depend upon the number in each category. Roughly, in duplicate the 100 score is due to NS not doubling 5♥s and gives them a deserved bottom, 300 both sides get an average and both have bid correctly finally 620 a shared top for NS because EWs have not had the whit to sacrifice. This also illustrates that the score you get in Duplicate depends upon the rest of the room. In Teams the results are more direct and dramatic, if you fail to sacrifice, they may gain 8 IMPs 620-300. If you are lucky and you make 4♠ s and they go two off not doubled in 5♥ s you gain 11 IMPs. Much more significant than Duplicate.

### 5.2.2 Pressure and Sacrifices

There are other classic cases where you decided to over bid your hand either for a sacrifice or simply to make it difficult for the opposition but it must be clear to your partner what you are doing so that it does not land you in a bad contract costing you 2% at Duplicate or perhaps the match in Teams. Some examples:

1♠ 1♥ P 2♣ 3♠ P P P

From the bidding it must be clear that the bidder is exceeding the value of his hand. In this example, the Opener bids 1♠ and guarantees to his partner that he has 12 points and at least 4♠s. One should also note that a bid implies a list of hands the Opener does not have. He does not have more than 19 HCPs, he does not have a balanced hand with 12-14 HCPs and he does not have single suited hand. 1♥ overcall tells everyone the Overcaller has 8 - 11 HCPs and a good 5 card suit as with 12-15 HCPs and a six card suit, he would have bid 2♥s and with 16+ HCPs he would have doubled. Clearly, the Overcaller could have more points and the right number of cards or the right number of points and more cards. No bidding system is perfect. The Responder passes showing less than 6 points. The Advancer bids 2♣s showing at least 5 ♣s, that he does not like ♥s and must have at least 12 HCPs. The Opener has a good ♠ suit and is weak in ♥s and ♣s so thinks he could make 8 tricks with a little help from his partner. 1 off doubled is better than letting the opposition make 3♥s or 4♣s so he bids 3♠s as a sacrifice. In this case Overcaller and Advancer declined to Double so the Opener has an easy ride. The Responder must not bid after the 3♠ bid because he knows from the bidding that the Opener must have over called his hand and was Sacrificing.

P 1♠ 2♥ P 4♥ P P P

Here the dealer passes and so his partner knows he has less than an opening hand. When he bids 4♥s, knowing that his partner has less than an opening, otherwise he would bid 2♥s, the Advancer has prevented the Opener from bidding 3♠s and is hoping for a modest loss of one or two tricks. The Overcaller cannot bid on.

1♠ 2♥ P 3♥ P P 3♠ ……

Here it is clear to the Opener that his partner is over bidding his hand as he passed the first time round so it must be a sacrifice.

1♠ 2♥ 3♣ P 3♦ P P 3♥ ……

The Opener and Responder don't like each other's suits and they have settled for ♦s but the Advancer has no defence against ♦s and almost enough for 3♥s, not enough as he passed the first opportunity so his 3♥ bid is a sacrifice.

***Your bids must be such that your partner can tell the difference between support and sacrifice.***

### 5.3 Negative Doubles

We can use the Negative Double (-veX), defined in Section 2.8, to help us in some of the above. The sequence 1♠ 2♥ takes away a lot of bidding space and makes it difficult for the Responder. Even the 1♠ opening bid is almost pre-emptive so the Responder needs help.

1♠ 2♥ X ....

The -ve double says I would have bid but for the interference from our opponent. Although this appears rather vague it does give the Opener reassurance that his partner has at least 6 HCPs and does not have 4 ♠s. He can now happily bid 2♠s showing 5♠s and 12-15 points. The Opener, with a minor and 16+ points, can now **reverse** with a bid of 3♣ /♦s as the partnership has at least 22 points which tells us we should be OK in a 3 level contract. Clearly, the -ve double has opened up a range of opportunities for the Opener and his partner; another example is

1♣ 1♥ X ...

as define here, the Responder will not have 4+♠s and 6+ points otherwise he would have bid it, he will not have 4+♦ and 10+ points otherwise he would have bid that and he does not have 6-9 HCPs and a stop in ♥ otherwise he would have bid 1NT. A lot of information conveyed by a single X. The auction continues but with a well informed Opener.

### 5.4 Doubles for Penalties

A tricky subject with one simple axiom:
*a double of a no trump bid is always for penalties*
The doubler has a balanced hand and his partnership has more points than the opposition. There is always an exception to a rule, I regard 1 of suit Pass 1NT X as a take out double as the 1NT bidder is not necessarily balanced, it is just a point count, 6-9 HCPs and a decline of the Opener's

48

suit. There is the Rule of 4 & 6 for low level penalties; I never use it and refer the reader to reference {5} in Appendix B.

Penalty doubles that are easier to get right are the conversion of a take out double to penalties, doubling a sacrifice and doubling a game contract. The bidding goes

> 3♦ Pass Pass X Pass ,

now its your turn but you have AKJx in ♦s , your sitting over 7♦s to the Q, few other points but your partner's opening hand has winners you pass for penalties and expect to get a top score. If you are vulnerable and they are not, bidding 3NT may be a better choice.

Another, must double for penalties, is when the opposition has clearly sacrificed and you do not have the strength to out bid them. This is simply minimising the damaged to your score. Finally, doubling a game contract where there are no apparent long suits with shortages, you have significant trumps over the long holding so you can count enough winners in you hand to defeat the contract. So be wary of doubling 5 in a minor contract as they are usually bid on the basis of long suits and shortages, the sort of hands that are unsuitable for NT. You hold the A of trumps and AK in another suit but this does not mean you are guaranteed 3 tricks against a 5 Level contract.

Contents

# Chapter 6 Defences in Bidding

## 6.1 Introduction

All defensive measures must be agreed with your partner, once again it is a team game. You have picked up your hand, checked its shape and counted its points so you are ready to go but your RHO bids one of the following: 1NT, 2♥, 2♠, 3♣/♦/♥/♠. They are all pre-emptive bids design to make it difficult for you to bid so you need a defence against each one. You may have to cope with 2♦, weak, or 2♦ Multi as well. We arm ourselves with bids to deal with each possibility; some elements I have already described but I shall cover them all here in the context of a pre-emptive bid.

## 6.2 Defence against weak 1NT
### 6.2.1 Astro Defence after 1NT opening.

There are a number of conventions for the defence against a 1NT opening such as Astro, As[p]tro, Landy, Cansino, Splash etc., but I prefer Astro. This can be used after a weak or strong 1NT opening bid. Here you only need 5:4 in two suits but always ensure you have 12 points when a fit is achieved with your partner. The 5:4 may be either way round. The bids are as follows:

> 1NT 2♣    5:4 in ♥s and a lower suit,
> 1NT 2♦    5:4 in ♠s and a lower suit,

but which suit contains 5 cards is unspecified. Let's consider the case when Responder passes 1NT 2♣ : with 4♥s, the Advancer bids ♥s at the appropriate level., with 3♥s she would like to know which suit is the 5 card suit and bids 2♦ . Overcaller bids either 3♣, ♦ (i.e. Pass) or 2♥s and the Advancer can pass all of them. With a hand containing 10 or more HCPs the Advancer should bid 2NT asking for the other suit. This gives the Advancer a complete picture of the Overcaller's hand that enables her to bid the right 3 or 4 Level contract. The pattern after the 2♦ Astro bid is the same. If the Advancer has a long suit in the conventionally bid suit she can break the convention and pass or raise the conventionally bid suit. Simple examples:

> 1NT 2♦  P 2♠ , at least 4♠ s but less than 9 points, maybe 0 &
> 1NT 2♣  2♦ (not a transfer) 3♥, at least 4 ♥ s and 10-12 points.

After 1NT bid by opponents most sequences are summarised in the table below:

| Overc'r 1 | Advancer | Overc'r 2 | Limits |
|---|---|---|---|
| 2♣ | 2♦ | 2♥ | 5 cards ♥ suit |
|  |  | 3♣ | 5 card ♣ suit |
|  |  | Pass | 5 card ♦ suit |
|  | 2♥ |  | 4 card ♥ suit and 0-9 points |
|  | 3♥ |  | 4 card ♥ suit and 10-12 points |
|  | 4♥ |  | 4 card ♥ suit and 13-18 points |
|  | 3NT* |  | 5:4 in ♠ s and another 13+ HCPs |
|  | 4NT |  | RKCB in ♥ s 20+ points |
|  | 2NT | 3♣ | 5 card suit. Adv.10+ HCPs < 3♥ s |
|  |  | 3♦ | 5 card suit. Adv.10+ HCPs < 3♥ s |
| 2♦ | 2♥ | 2♠ | 5 cards ♠ suit |
|  |  | 3♣ | 5 card ♣ suit |
|  |  | 3♦ | 5 card ♦ suit |
|  |  | Pass | 5 card ♥ suit |
|  | 2♠ |  | 4 card ♠ suit and 0-9 points |
|  | 3♠ |  | 4 card ♠ suit and 10-12 points |
|  | 4♠ |  | 4 card ♠ suit and 13-18 points |
|  | 3NT |  | 5:4 in ♠ s and another 13+ HCPs |
|  | 4NT |  | RKCB in ♠ s 20+ points |
|  | 2NT | 3♣ | 5 card suit. Adv.10+ HCPs < 3♠ s |
|  |  | 3♦ | 5 card suit. Adv.10+ HCPs < 3♠ s |
|  |  | 3♥ | 5 card suit. Adv.10+ HCPs < 3♠ s |

When the Advancer bids 2NT and Overcaller detects the pair has game points, she has to raise her bids a level to show this to her partner.

### 6.2.2 Suit Overcalls.

If you have a hand suitable for a normal overcall in ♥s or ♠s then you can simply bid it.
1NT 2♥ ….
The 2♥ bid shows you have 12-15 HCPs and a good 6 card suit. Similarly 1NT 3♥ ..
shows a 7 card suit and 6-9 HCPs: but what about 3♣s and 3♦s, we cannot bid 2♣ as an overcall as it is reserved for Astro so we adapt our overcalls to fit the context, not a popular approach with me as I like bids to have one

meaning regardless of the context. We use 3♣s and 3♦s to indicated a standard 2 Level overcall.
1NT 3♦ ...
The 3♦ bid indicates 12-15 HCPs and a good 6 card suit. Now what do we do with the 3♦ pre-empt? With a 8 card suit and 6-9 HCPs, I would bid 4♦s but with a weak, 7 card hand, I would temper my bid by the vulnerability. This last comment should be taken as a universal comment where you have to consider what happens if you go off both doubled and not doubled.

### 6.2.3 Doubles and Defences

We still have Doubles,X , Unusual 2NT and Michael's Cue bid in our arsenal. We cannot use Michaels Cue bid as we have no suit to bid. Using a double, X

> 1NT X ...

This bid connects with the claim that the double of NT is always for penalties and shows at least 15 HCPs and a balanced hand. Now the Advancer may have 10 HCPs and a balanced hand so if they are non vulnerable and we are vulnerable and can make 9 tricks in 3NT, the score are as follows: 1NT X 3 off, we get 500 points but 3NT making, we get 600 points. In a competitive environment, it is rare for 1NT X to be left in as you opponents will have some defence against this, see Section 5.7.2.

The use of an unusual 2NT against a 1NT opening is straight forward:

> 1NT 2NT ..

The Overcaller needs to be at least 5:5 in the minors and have at least 10 HCPs, the Advancer bids his longest minor at an appropriate level. If the Overcaller had a balanced hand with 15 or more points he would simply X so there is no possibility that the 2NT call is natural.

### 6.3 Defence against weak 2's

The fashion has swung all the way to three weak twos, 2♦ /♥ /♠ s, as opening bids so we have to have a defence against all three. The simple advice given is X if you have an opening hand which is rather low key advice so I have devised a more complete approach that has similarities to Astro. This keeps life fairly simple. Consider your hand and divide it into five possibilities: a standard 2 level overcall, a 5:4 hand (at least should always be attached to the 5:4 or 5/4) with 10+ HCPs, a balanced opening hand with 12-15 HCPs, a hand with 16+ HCPs or finally none of the above. Dealing with the last hand, none of the above, is the simplest: Pass.

### 6.3.1 Standard 2 Level overcall available

It is reasonable to assume we do not want to play in their 6 card suit so the bidding is affected by the opening bid. With a standard 2 level overcall bid available, bid it at the 2 level if possible but at the three level if the 2 level is blocked. With a balanced 12-15 hand or 16+ HCPs X. This leaves us with the 5:4 hands where we need to define a bid to tell our partner which pair we have and that we have 10+ HCPs.

### 6.3.2 Showing a 5:4 hand.

Lets assume they open 2♥, weak, clearly a 2♠ overcall is available and we may also consider 5:4 in ♣ :♠ , ♣ :♦ , and ♦ :♠ so we would like a bid for each. Keeping almost in line with the Unusual 2NT we define 2NT as 5:4 in the minors, 3♣ as 5:4 in ♣ & ♠ s and 3♦ as 5:4 in ♦ and ♠ s. In line with these definitions we devalue the 2♠ overcall to 12-15 HCPs and a good 5 cards suit. We can create a complete set of bids by making 3♥s, asking for a stop for 3NT and 3♠ a strong hand with a good 6 card spade suit.

This is a complete defence against a weak 2 opening of 2♥ s which we can adjust for both a weak 2♠ s and with a little more adjustment as a defence against a weak 2♦ . Against a weak 2♠ we have lost the 2 level 2♥ overcall. The 2NT bid remains the same and 3♣ and 3♦ shows hearts and the minor instead of spades but 3♥ becomes a standard 2 level overcall: 12-15 HCPs and a good 6 card suit. 3♠ s has the expected meaning of asking for a stopper in spades for 3NT.

The weak 2♦ opening means we don't want to play in ♦s but we have more bids available, i.e. 2♦s is not very pre-emptive. We can use our devalued 2 level overcall in both ♥s and ♠ s but 2NT in line with the Unusual 2NT bid, becomes the two lowest un-bid suits, ♣s and ♥s, but could be 5:4. 3♣ follows a similar pattern as ♣s and ♠s, as we have already covered the ♣s and ♥s with the 2NT bid, whilst 3♦s is asking for a stopper and 3♥s and 3♠s are strong bids with a good 6 card suit.

These definitions and choices can presented in tabular form:
After they bid weak 2♦ / 2♥ / 2♠:

| Open | 2ⁿᵈ seat | meaning |
|---|---|---|
| 2♦ | 2♥ | 5♥, SQ7, 12-15 HCP can have 4♠ |
|  | 2♠ | 5♠, SQ7, 12-15 HCP can have 4♥ |
|  | 2NT | 5♣ & 4♥ 12-15 HCP |
|  | 3♣ | 5♣ & 4♠ 12-15 HCP |
|  | 3♦ | 16+ HCP, asking stop NT, or a suit |
|  | 3♥ | 6 cards 16+ HCP |
|  | 3♠ | 6 cards 16+ HCP |
|  | 3NT | 19+ HCP control all suits |
|  | X | None of the above. 12+ points, take out, forcing |
|  | Pass | None of the above |
| 2♥ | 2♠ | 5♠, SQ7, 12-15 HCP |
|  | 2NT | ♣ & ♦ 5/4 12-15 HCP |
|  | 3♣ | ♣ & ♠ 5/4 12-15 HCP |
|  | 3♦ | ♦ & ♠ 5/4 12-15 HCP |
|  | 3♥ | 16+ HCP asking for stop NT or a suit |
|  | 3♠ | 6 cards 16+ hcp |
|  | 3NT | 19+ HCP control all suits |
|  | X | None of the above. 12+ points, take out, forcing |
|  | Pass | None of the above |
| 2♠ | 2NT | ♣ & ♦ 5/4 12-15 HCP |
|  | 3♣ | ♣ & ♥ 5/4 12-15 HCP |
|  | 3♦ | ♦ & ♥ 5/4 12-15 HCP |
|  | 3♥ | 6♥ card, SQ8, 12+ HCP |
|  | 3♠ | 16+ HCP asking for stop NT or a suit |
|  | 3NT | 19+ HCP control all suits |
|  | X | None of the above. 12+ points, take out, forcing |
|  | Pass | None of the above |

### 6.4 Defence against Multi 2 Diamond

Fortunately, this does not come up very often as the defence can become very complicated because the opening contains so many options therefore it is better to stick to something similar to the defence against weak 2s. The Overcaller should ignore the bid and pass on as much information to his partner as possible using similar techniques to the defence against weak 2s. If you are not familiar with Section 6.3, I suggest you re-read it now and then come back to this. We can jump to the tabular form using our ideas from weak 2s above:

| Opener | Overcaller | Meaning |
|---|---|---|
| Multi 2♦ | 2♥ | 5 ♥s and 12-15 HCP |
|  | 2♠ | 5♠s and 12-15 HCP |
|  | 2NT | 5/4 ♣ & ♦ 12-15 HCP |
|  | 3♣ | 6♣ 12-15 HCP |
|  | 3♦ | 6♦ 12-15 HCP |
|  | 3♥ | 6♥ 12-15 HCP |
|  | 3♠ | 6♠ 12-15 HCP |
|  | 3NT | Balanced 22+ |
|  | X | None of the above & 12 + HCP. For take out including NT |
|  | Pass | None of the above |

When the bidding goes:

2♦ (alert) Pass 2♥ ( alert) or 2NT ( alert) ..

The Advancer has choices based upon the bids so far. 2♥ is a pass or correct bid from a weak hand but opener maybe strong. The Advancer can X saying ♥s is my suit or bid from the table above except the final X. If the Responder bids 2NT, this is an indication of a strong hand and is asking the Opener for more information with most hands Advancer should pass.

### 6.5 Defence against Doubles and Michael's Cue Bid

You have opened 1 of a suit and the Overcaller Doubles, X. Your

partner wants to block the Advancer if possible so bids a new suit with the normal rules but if he has 4 cards in your bid suit he uses the **stretch raise**.
The bidding goes 1♦ X :
2♦ shows 4 ♦ s and 0-5 points
2NT shows 4♦ s and 10-12 points
3♦ shows 4♦ s and 6-9 points

With 13 HCPs the Responder might bid 3NT provided he has stops in the three un-bid suits.

You have opened 1♥ and they have bid 2♥ s as a Michael's Cue bid. Your partner, the Responder, with 4 ♥ s can bid a **stretch raise**, 2NT indicating a normal raise to 3♥ , bid 3♥ s to show a normal raise to 2♥ s and X to indicate a weak hand as the Responder has lost the 2 Level bid because Michaels bidder has taken it away.

## 6.6 Defence against Weak 3 or more Opening Bids

These are the traditional pre-emptive openings but the strength and suit guarantees may vary wildly so the Overcaller should always ask the Responder what strength and length are guaranteed and whether there are any further conditions on outside suits or honour cards. For example, you may get the answer a 7 card suit with 6-9 HCPs and no other conditions but you may also get it could be a 6 card suit with 3-10 HCPs and does not have a four card major. Our defence is based upon the middle ground of the first answer: 6-9 HCPs and a 7 card suit.

How you respond depends upon whether you are in the 2nd seat (Overcaller) or the 4th seat (Advancer). A pre-empt at the 3 level leaves you very little bidding room to discover your best contract and is therefore more effective than a weak 2 opening. You must consider the two attributes of your hand and take some risks. I shall start in the 2nd seat and reverse my approach compared to defending against a weak 2.

### 6.6.1 2nd Seat:

Do you have at least 12-15 points and a 4432 or 4441 with no more than 2 cards in the bid suit. Is your 3 card suit strong, if so double, X, asking your partner to pick a suit. If the Responder passes this, it becomes a forcing bid and the Advancer must bid his longest suit or highest rank with equal length suits.

With 16+ HCPs, a long minor, at least 6 cards, and two cards with a stopper in the suit bid, then bid 3NT. In the bid suit this would typically be Kx or Ax but may be Qxx. Risky but one you must take after a 3 level pre-empt.

With a balanced hand, 18+ HCPs and a stopper in the bid suit has the same potential as the long minor so bid 3NT.

With 16 HCPs and 5/6 cards in a suit and no stop in the pre-empt suit, bid 3 or 4 in the suit respectively.

You can also use other devices such as Unusual 4NT and Michaels Cue bid. Let's take them in turn, with 16+ HCPs and 5:5 in the two lowest un-bid suits you can bid 4NT ( you can't bid 3NT as that would be to play) which inevitably leads you to a game contract in a minor or hearts. This is less risky than it appears as with a fit you will have at least 20 points and you are only looking for 9 points from your partner. Looking at it another way, the pre-emptor typically has 7 HCPs and you have 16 leaving 17 split between the other two hand so your partner will average 8 HCPs. you must have at least 1 shortage point so we have reach an average of 29 points for the pair of hands and a 5 level contract has a good chance of making. Michaels can only be used against a minor suit pre-empt otherwise you may push the bidding into an un-makable small slam.

As ever if you have none of these hands pass and be prepared to defend.

### 6.6.2 4th Seat.

With no bid by the Overcaller or Responder, you have become the Protective bidder and should add three points to your hand and use the bids laid out for the 2nd set.

Contents

# Chapter 7 Must Knows, before playing a hand.

Description of the play of the cards has to follow consideration of the bidding because how you play the cards depends upon the bidding. Before the auction starts make sure you know the bidding system the opposition is using. At the completion of the auction, the person on lead may ask questions of the bidders about the meaning and implications of their bids. These questions are answered by the receiver of the bid not the giver. When the person on lead is content, she choses a card to lead and places it face down on the table. Now is the opportunity for the leader's partner to ask questions until she is satisfied. When the questions are complete, the leader turns over the card, "faces the card." This chapter concentrates on things you must do whether you are defending or declarer and whether you are playing a no trump or a trump contract. You need to do this at the start of every hand.

## 7.1 The Auction

Consider an uncontested auction, the bidding goes 1NT Pass 3NT followed by three passes. This looks unhelpful but lets analyse what it tells us. The Opener, playing weak 1NT, has 12-14 HCPs is balanced and does not contain a 5 card major. The Responder has 13+ HCPs and does not have a 4 card major otherwise she would have bid 2♣ , Stayman. With no other information we can assume the Defenders have about 7 HCPs each and the Overcaller certainly does not have a good 6 card suit and 10 HCPs or a 5:4 and 10 HCPs suitable for a defence, against a weak 1NT, such as Astro. I shall return to examples of more auctions and what they tell us. Let s assume you lead a K form KQJx , I shall discuss leads in Section 9.4.1. You can now see Dummy and your own hand so you can now consider where the cards are you can't see; this is referred to as the split of the cards.

## 7.2 The split of the cards*

It is possible to play a decent hand of bridge without any knowledge of probabilities, so you may ignore this section if you wish.

| Probable Division of Cards |||
|---|---|---|
| Cards Outstanding | Division | Probability % |
| 2 | 1:1 | 52 |
|   | 2:0 | 48 |
| 3 | 2:1 | 78 |
|   | 0:3 | 22 |
| 4 | 1:3 | 50 |
|   | 2:2 | 41 |
| 5 | 2:3 | 68 |
|   | 1:4 | 28 |
| 6 | 2:4 | 48 |
|   | 3:3 | 36 |
| 7 | 3:4 | 62 |
|   | 2:5 | 31 |
| 8 | 3:5 | 47 |
|   | 4:4 | 33 |

Whether Declarer or Defender, after the first lead is made you can see two hands so for each suit you can decide on the split of the cards you can't see using the auction and standard probabilities. I have given a list above of the probabilities commonly used and a complete set can be found in {9}. For the complete mathematical theory, you may consult {10}. The above table only applies to suits about which you have no information. When you have information from the auction, use that first, see Section 7.3. Notice an even number of cards you cannot see is likely to split in an unequal fashion. A common occurrence is you are playing in NTs with 7 cards between the two hands and you hold AKQx so if you always play them off the top you will make 4 tricks 36% of the time, as the split is most likely to be 4:2, therefore this is not the best approach. An example of this is:

| Q65 | AKT8 |

Play the A first in case the J is a singleton, followed by 8 to the Q, watch the cards involuntary played by the opposition. Clearly if the J is part of a doubleton, it falls and you make four tricks. However, very often they play the 2, 3, 4 and 7 and you have no idea where the 9 and J are. Watching the cards played by the opposition is important as you may find in this example one opponent plays the 7 followed by the 2, telling his partner he only has two cards in this suit. Thank you very much, I now know where the J and 9 are. If they both play low-high, you could go for a 3:3 split but they could be just shrewd opponents who are not telling you anything. You have to play the 6 and your opponent plays the 9, you are still no wiser about where the J is but it is now a 50:50 choice. At this point I would play the J as it is still more likely that one opponent started with 4 cards in the suit and you know which one has at least 3 so he is more likely to have 4. The real alternative is to try to place the suit lengths after the lead has been faced using the auction, the cards you can see and the table of probabilities above. The table also suggest that with an 8 cards suit and the top three honours, playing for a 3:2 split is the best approach.

### 7.3 A complex auction*

This section may be skipped over on your first reading. Now let's consider a contested auction:

| 1♦ 1♥ 1♠ 2♥ 3♣ P 3NT P P |

The dealer is S so the contract is 3NT by N. This gives us a lot of information and we must also consider it before playing a card. N is the declarer, you are sitting E and so you must lead but first you consider the auction. You have 10 points with 3♥ s and your partner has a good 5 card ♥ suit and at least 8 HCPs. What else do you know; in turn S initially shows at least 12 points and a 4 card ♦ suit, N has a 4 card ♠ suit and at least 6 HCPs ; S's second bid shows at least 16 points as she is prepared to bid at the 3 level ( this requires a combined 22 points at least, 16+6) and shows 5♦ s and 4♣ s. N decides they have enough for 3NT, with at least 9 points, and has two stoppers in ♥ s. You have significant information about all four hands.

We have to use the information about suits from the auction.

The bidding marks S with 5♦s and 4♣s but as she has passed 3NT and is likely to have a [2254] hand whereas N has at least 4♠s and 2 ♥s and does not like ♣ or ♦s so will be perhaps have a [5323] hand. W has [-5--] and E [-3--] . E is on lead and lets say her hand is [4324], Dummy is [2254] and W is likely to have 2♠s, 4♦s and 2♣s making it a [2542]. So we have S [2254], W [2542], N [5323] and E [4324], surprise surprise each suit adds up to 13. S has a stronger hand than N and each have controls in 2 suits. The bidding of the hands: E bid 2♥s with 9 HCPs and a doubleton, whilst S only had 15 HCPs, suggest declarer has only 24 HCPs points and no suit longer than 7 cards, she is in trouble.

This information to be used in the play of the hand but the lead should be your highest ♥ as your partner has a good ♥ suit and wants to judge which hearts are in N.

*At the end of the auction mentally tick off what you know.*
*After seeing Dummy add to what you know.*

### 7.4 Keeping track of the cards.

A major part of play is keeping track of the cards that have been played and the remaining length in each hand. A few people find this inordinately easy and make very good card players. The rest of us mortals have to work at it and you may find it easier to focus on the honours left and the length in you opponents hands of important suits. This is true whether you are declarer or defender and whether the contract is a suit or NT contract. Your assessment of each hand gives you a picture of each hand and as the cards are played you can tick them off. This enables you to chose the right card at the right time.

As we have seen above, your opponents may inadvertently give you clues about their holding during the play. Make sure you know their discard system so you can use it to your advantage. Watch for an unforced honour card dropping as it always indicates a shortage in that suit.

### 7.5 Finesse or Drop

When playing a hand we can use probabilities to give us some hope of making the right choice. An outline is given below with the evidence again from {9}.

## *When Your Opponents Start With*

| | |
|---|---|
| 2 cards | Play for the drop, since there is a chance that the king will fall. If you have AK, you have no interest in this. |
| 3 or 4 cards | Finesse against the king, but not against the queen or jack. The chance of dropping a bare king is well below 50% in both cases, whereas the chance of dropping a singleton or doubleton queen is 78% when three cards are out and 53% when four cards are out. |
| 5 or 6 cards | Finesse against the king or queen but not against the jack. The chance of dropping a singleton or doubleton queen has fallen below 50% |
| 7 or 8 cards | Finesse against the king, queen or jack. The chance of bringing down the jack in three rounds has fallen well below 50% in both cases. |

Please don't turn these into mantras. You still have to combine them with all the evidence from the auction and the likely split. Where you are unsure it is better to play other suits where honour cards will have to drop so that you have more information about the likely location of the remaining honours. The lead may also indicate a strong suit in one hand so the remaining strength should be in the fourth hand.

A classic problem for the Declarer is having AJxx in one hand and KTxx in the other and with no information from opponents which way to finesse it is a 50% guess. This is a double **tenace**, where a tenace is a pair of cards you can use to carry out a finesse. One can try to leave this suit to last and use the cards played to improve your odds of making the correct finesse. If you find the remaining cards are unevenly split, 4:1, you should assume the card you want to finesse is in the longer hand. However, if an overcall has shown there are very few points in one hand you must finesse through the overcaller.

A common problem is Dummy has AJT9x you have 3 cards in the same suit in your hand and you have no information on the split of the suit strength between your opponents. You lead towards Dummy and the LHO plays low and you put up the 9 which is beaten by the K or Q. If the K appears there is some chance RHO does not have the Q but no guarantee. You win the next trick and play to the same suit in Dummy, and LHO plays low so you now put up the T. This is known as playing for split honours based upon the concept that the points are split and so they will also split in suits with no overcall in the auction. The odds now change because we have a 9 card suit with 3 cards in the opponents hands. The probabilities at each level are too numerous to remember so stick to the original values: 3 cards out split 2:1 78% of the time. I shall return to this example in Chapter 8 on the play of the cards.

Consider the auction:

1♣ 2♥ 2♠ P 4♠ P P P

As Declarer you ask the Advancer what the meaning of the 2♥ jump overcall is and get the reply, "intermediate with a good 6 card suit." You inspect your hand and Dummy and find you have 26 HCPs, add to this 12 for Overcaller which leaves 2 for the Advancer and surprise of the century the Advancer leads the Q♥ . This places all the honours you can't see with the Overcaller and you can finesse where you need to.

When you have no information from the auction, you can only rely on the tables above. The examples of card play here are only to illustrate the need for a knowledge of the likely splits and the distribution of points. I shall treat card play more generally in Chapters 8 & 9.

### 7.6 The Knowledge you need

Whether you are declarer or a defender playing in a suit or NT, here are the crucial things you need to do:

*Remember the auction*
*Note the lead*
*Estimate the splits*
*Keep track of the cards*
*Finesse or Drop*

Contents

## Chapter 8 Playing as Declarer

This is the easiest part of the game, you have control of two hands, your are equipped with all the knowledge laid out in Chapter 7 and you are on your own. For once it is not a team game. There are two different types of contract, either no trumps or a suit contract and each plays a little differently. Many hands "play themselves," that is the position of tenaces are fixed, regardless of where the strength is, and long suits establish themselves so you have to play the cards and gain an average score. We have to concentrate on hands where the prior knowledge and play can make a difference to the outcome.

When deciding your plan there are essentially 7 well known types of hand:

*Ruffing in the short side, usually Dummy*
*Establishing a long suit, turning low spot cards into winners*
*Using finesses*
*Discarding losers*
*Duck and ruff*
*The cross ruff*
*Relying on squeezes and end plays\**

I shall consider each of these along with our knowledge of the cards and points together with a few techniques. For a more detailed approach to deduction consult {11}.

Many times at the end of a hand your partner will say you should have done A, B and C and my question has always been, " how could I have known that with the information I had at the beginning of the hand?" Too often the answer is a blank look because it is a comment based upon 20:20 hindsight. My advice is Dummy should only congratulate or commiserate with their partner at the end of a hand. If your partner plays a particular combination of cards badly several times, I would suggest putting an explanation on paper or in an email and discussing it with your partner.

## 8.1 Declarer playing in No Trumps.

### 8.1.1 What do you learn from the lead

The first step is that your LHO makes a lead. You should ask yourself the question, what does it tell me. Well, you should ask the leader's partner if they use standard leads and you often get one of three replies: I don't know, yes or no and an explanation. With the first answer you assume they do use standard leads and these are given on a bidding card, see Appendix E page 3. Leads are different against NT and suit contracts as the opposition is looking to establish a long suit and make tricks with low value cards that cannot be ruffed. A further consequence of this is that they may under lead an ace or a broken sequence which they would never do against a trump contract.

Against a 5 level contract, it is recommended that you lead an ace if you have one whether it is supported or not. This is based upon the assumption that 5 level contracts occur because the bidders are distributional and may well discard your suit containing an ace so that you never get to make it.

You should also consider the suit and answer the question why did he lead that suit. Often it is the unbid suit or an unbid major and you should use the likely splits to estimate the suit length together with the value of the suit played. For example if the card led is the 4♠s and you play the K♠ and RHO plays the 5♠ and you can't see the 2♠ , it is very likely with the LHO and he led from a 5 card suit rather than a four card suit. However, more mental effort is required before you play the first card from Dummy. In the next section, the suit splits and point distribution are considered using this initial card play. This will show you that to play the K was fatal and emphasises that you must consider everything before playing the first card.

Sometimes the lead says little about the leader's holding as it is a lead through strength. This is more important for Defender play but should not be ignored as Declarer, on either the first lead or later leads, it makes sense to lead through a perceived strength. What does this mean? The weakest case is that when Dummy was biding, he bid a suit denied by his partner , later to become Declarer, e.g.

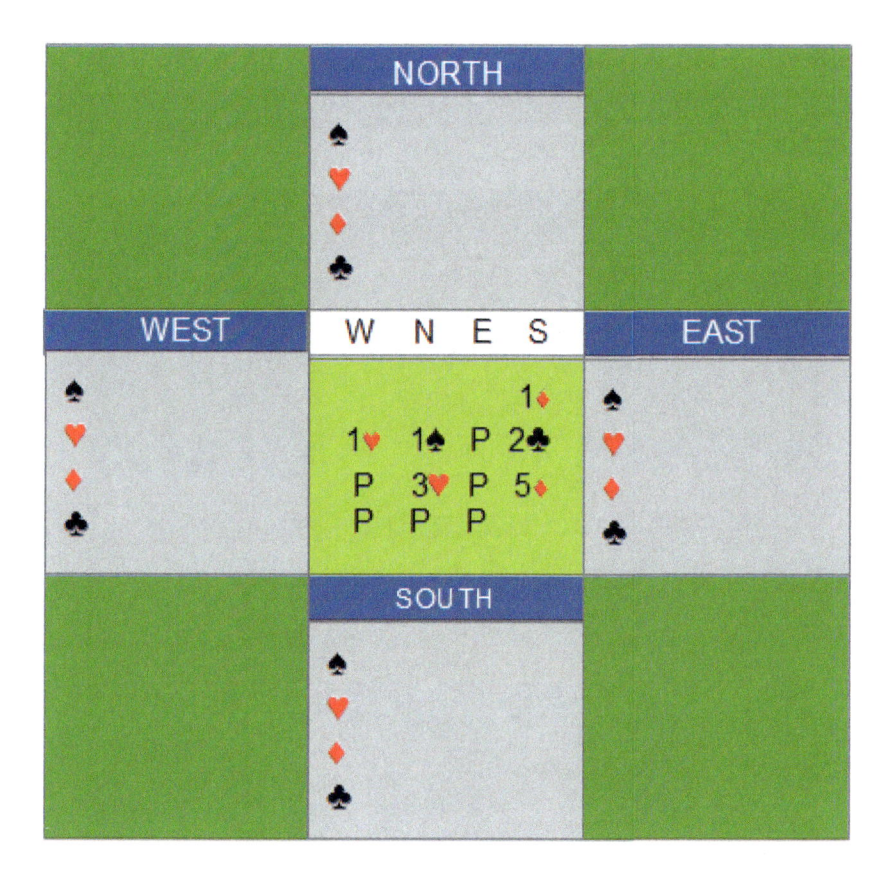

|   |   |   |   |
|---|---|---|---|
|   | NORTH ♠ ♥ ♦ ♣ |   |   |
| WEST ♠ ♥ ♦ ♣ | W N E S<br>　 　 　 1♦<br>1♥ 1♠ P 2♣<br>P 3♥ P 5♦<br>P P P | EAST ♠ ♥ ♦ ♣ |   |
|   | SOUTH ♠ ♥ ♦ ♣ |   |   |

Here the declarer can use the auction, 1♥ overcall and the lead, to understand the EW hands. The 3♥ bid is forth suit forcing, asking for a stop in ♥s, S not having a stop but a better than minimum hand chooses 5♦s as the contract. W leads a low ♠ hoping his partner has his 3 HCPs as the K♠s. With the bidding and the lead, declarer knows where all the HCPs are and plays the hand accordingly.

### 8.1.2 Splits and Card counting*

If you are not of a scientific bent then you might like to skip this section, it is even a little heavy for the scientific Newcomer but useful. We must give more time to the question of splits and the make up of the two hands of the opponents. The lead has shown the Defenders have an interest in one suit but what about the others. You should consider the likely split of each suit based upon the cards in your own hand and Dummy. To this you can add information from their bids if they made any and this enables you to get an approximate description of their hands.

Consider a typical hand:

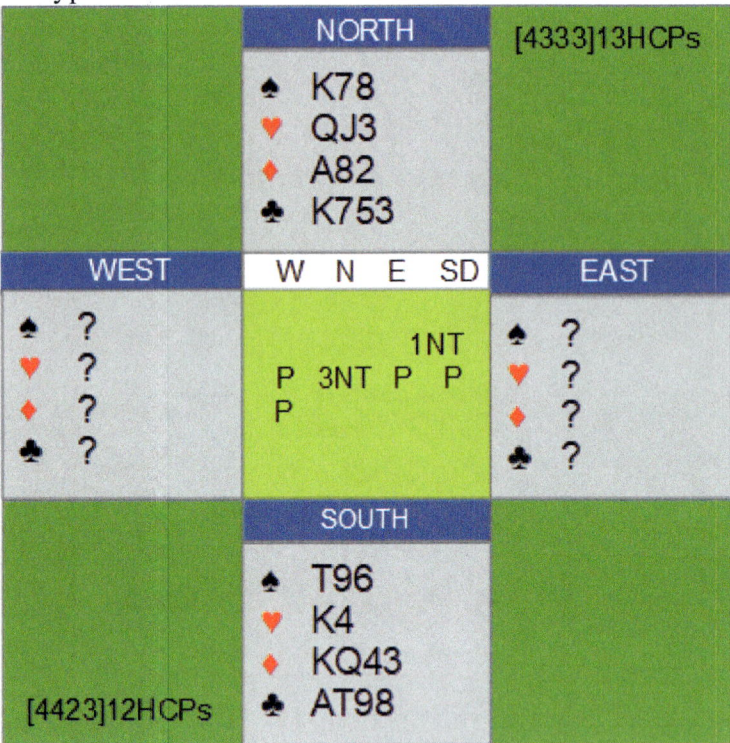

|  | NORTH | [4333]13HCPs |
|---|---|---|
|  | ♠ K78<br>♥ QJ3<br>♦ A82<br>♣ K753 |  |
| WEST | W  N  E  SD | EAST |
| ♠ ?<br>♥ ?<br>♦ ?<br>♣ ? |       1NT<br>P 3NT P  P<br>P | ♠ ?<br>♥ ?<br>♦ ?<br>♣ ? |
|  | SOUTH |  |
| [4423]12HCPs | ♠ T96<br>♥ K4<br>♦ KQ43<br>♣ AT98 |  |

I shall use the diagram above repeatedly so let consider its layout. I have drawn this in a 3X3 matrix where the centre square header gives the player positions round the table and the D refers to dealer not declarer. The centre square contains the bidding. I shall add V to pairs of positions to indicate vulnerable when necessary. No one is vulnerable in this example. The hands are given below the table positions and the next square, clockwise, from the hand gives its distribution [♣ ♦ ♥ ♠ ] and its strength in points or HCPs. Clearly, S, the dealer has a [4423] balanced hand and 12 HCPs and N has a [4333] balanced hand with 13 HCPs. The bidding goes 1NT P 3NT P P P and the lead from W is the 5♠ as in Section 8.1.1 above. You have asked

68

your questions and must now make your estimate of the opponents hands. The lead and RHO opponents play suggest W has a five card ♠ suit although 4:3 would have been more likely. This places the ♠s as 5:2. With 8 ♥s out the most likely split is 3:5 placing the shorter part with W to counteract the 5 card ♠ suit. There are 6 ♦ s out and we place these as 2:4. Finally, ♣ s can be placed as 3:2. This gives W a [3235] and E a [2452] hand. There are 15 HCPs missing and we give 8 to W and 7 to E as W has a potentially strong suit is ♠ s. We can redraw the matrix placing the hand distributions and strengths in the corners and putting the number of cards in each suit in () next to the suit symbol.

|  | NORTH | [4333]13HCPs |
|---|---|---|
|  | ♠ K78<br>♥ QJ3<br>♦ A82<br>♣ K753 |  |
| [3235] 8HCPs |  |  |
| WEST | W  N  E  SD | EAST |
| ♠ (5)<br>♥ (3)<br>♦ (2)<br>♣ (3) |         1NT<br>P  3NT  P  P<br>P | ♠ (2)<br>♥ (5)<br>♦ (4)<br>♣ (2) |
|  | SOUTH | [2452] 7HCPs |
|  | ♠ T96<br>♥ K4<br>♦ KQ43<br>♣ AT98 |  |
| [4423]12HCPs |  |  |

Now consider the missing honours: AQJ ♠ s, A♥ s, J♦ s and QJ ♣ s.

The longer suit is likely to contain more honours (backed by probability theory) so we can place AQ♠ s with W, A♥ with E and Q♣ with W giving him 8 HCPs and the J♠, J♦ and J♣ s with E giving him 7 HCPs. If W had the AQJ♠ s, the lead would have been the Q, top of a broken sequence. Whether you place the J with W and the Q with E makes little difference.

This gives us:

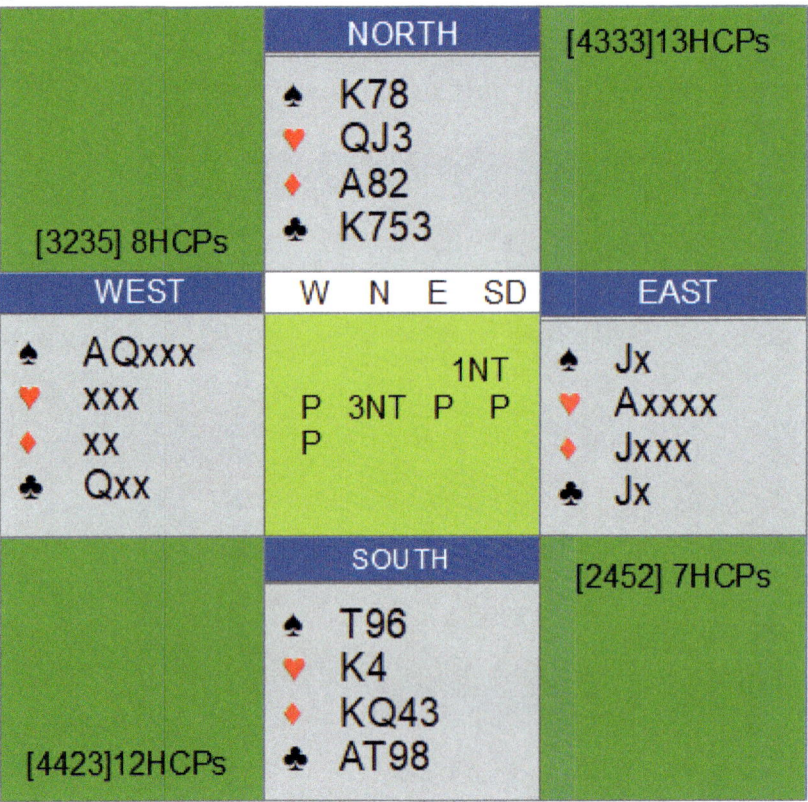

|  | NORTH | [4333]13HCPs |
|---|---|---|
| [3235] 8HCPs | ♠ K78<br>♥ QJ3<br>♦ A82<br>♣ K753 |  |
| WEST | W  N  E  SD | EAST |
| ♠ AQxxx<br>♥ xxx<br>♦ xx<br>♣ Qxx |       1NT<br>P 3NT P  P<br>P | ♠ Jx<br>♥ Axxxx<br>♦ Jxxx<br>♣ Jx |
|  | SOUTH | [2452] 7HCPs |
| [4423]12HCPs | ♠ T96<br>♥ K4<br>♦ KQ43<br>♣ AT98 |  |

Now we can consider the likely outcome after playing the K♠ s on the first trick. You can make 1♠ , 2♥ s ,4♦ s, and 3♣ s, 10 tricks, but to do so you must lose the lead twice and on the first time via the Q♣ s or the A♥ s, they take 4♠ tricks taking the contract two off. Instead of playing the K♠ before considering the picture of the hand, we can assume from the lead that W has a good 4 card ♠ suit and create the following picture:

|  | NORTH | [4333]13HCPs |
|---|---|---|
| [3244] 8HCPs | ♠ K78<br>♥ QJ3<br>♦ A82<br>♣ K753 | |
| WEST | W  N  E  SD | EAST |
| ♠ AQxx<br>♥ xxxx<br>♦ xx<br>♣ Qxx |          1NT<br>P  3NT  P  P<br>P | ♠ Jxx<br>♥ Axxx<br>♦ Jxxx<br>♣ Jx |
|  | SOUTH | [2443] 7HCPs |
| [4423]12HCPs | ♠ T96<br>♥ K4<br>♦ KQ43<br>♣ AT98 | |

Now you must play low from Dummy on the first trick and mark W as the danger hand. They can now make 3 ♠ tricks and a ♥ so you cannot afford to lose a ♣ trick. W is unlikely to have 2 aces otherwise he would have overcalled the 1NT opening bid so later you should lose to the ace of ♥ s in E. What does E play after taking the first trick with the J♠s ? I shall consider this example in Defender play in Chapter 9 but here lets consider E's four options: play a low ♠ , play the A♥s , play a low ♦ , or play J ♣s . In reverse order, playing the J♣s , marks W with the Q and S takes the trick with A and plays the T towards the K and makes 4 ♣ tricks. Leading a ♥ or ♦ makes life difficult for declarer.

    As the play of the hand continues, you should count the cards played by each defender and try to keep track of all the denominations. From this you can modify your picture of the two defending hands so that your end play is the most likely to gain the maximum number of tricks.

### 8.1.3 Check their system.

You should check what system of signals and discards your opponents are using as this will give you more information about their hands. I shall cover this topic in more detail in Chapter 9 so you may wish to flit back and forth between the two Chapters at this stage. In NT your RHO may give an encourage or discourage signal on the first lead. An encourage signal, high card, may also be an unblocking manoeuvrer from your RHO so your estimate of the cards in each hand enables you to decide whether you think they have two or more cards in the suit. If your RHO gives a discourage, low card signal , you must consider what else your opponents have and there are two distinct possibilities either the leader has everything that you don't have or your RHO has a different strong suit he would like led. Of course there is a third possibility that the leader has nothing and would be happy not to lead but lead he must. These early indicators are often the crucial key to success so you must be very careful on the first trick. You must try to work out, from the first card card played, the best card to play from Dummy and from the third card played how to play the rest of the hand. Once playing against a pair of internationals, at the end of the round, my RHO turned to my partner and said, "you must be the fastest declarer in the West." My partner and I both smiled gently and politely waved them goodbye but we both accepted it was a calculated insult. My partner was inclined to play the first trick thoughtlessly and then stop and think about the hand. He was an extremely nice guy but an average Bridge player just like me; we spent many happy years playing Bridge together.

### 8.1.4 Count your winners and note your Controls

The next step is to count your top winners, ones that if you play all your cards top down, you are guaranteed to make, not a good way to play them. Typically, you may have 6 when you are playing in 3NT needing 9 tricks. Now you have to consider where am I going to get three extra tricks from. First look at you longest suit, rarely above 8 cards but sometimes it is. In that suit how many tricks can you make when losing one finesse whilst maintaining controls in all the other suits. If this adds 3 tricks you have found a quick solution. It is rarely that easy. Here is an example but defenders will do their best to thwart your plan.

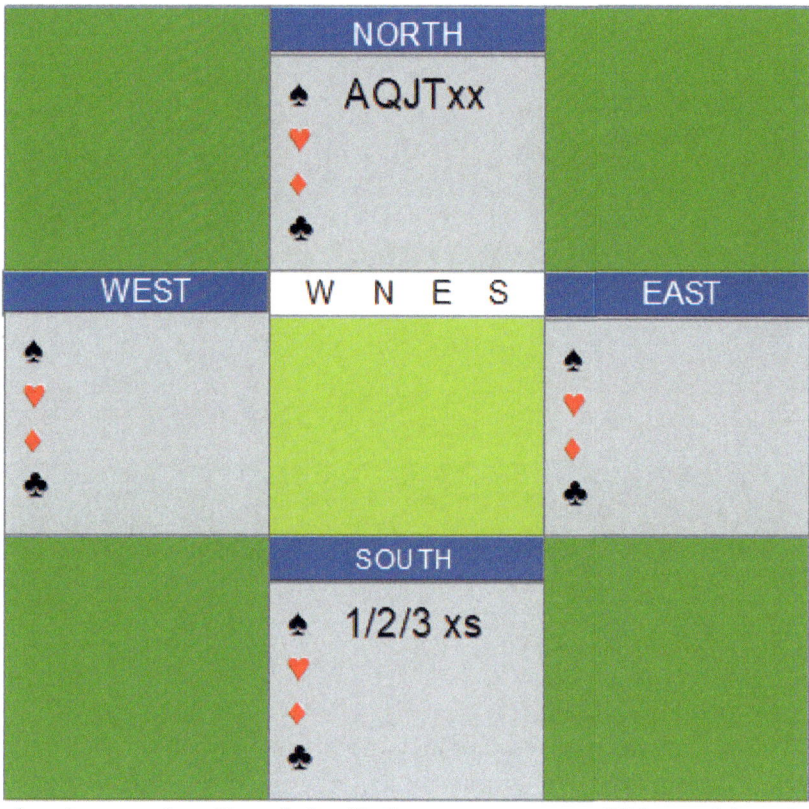

|  | NORTH |  |
|---|---|---|
|  | ♠ AQJTxx<br>♥<br>♦<br>♣ |  |
| WEST<br>♠<br>♥<br>♦<br>♣ | W  N  E  S | EAST<br>♠<br>♥<br>♦<br>♣ |
|  | SOUTH |  |
|  | ♠ 1/2/3 xs<br>♥<br>♦<br>♣ |  |

You play low to the Q and the K does not appear. This problem is very common, so it is worth considering in detail. There are three attributes you need to consider: can you afford to lose one trick and still make your contract, how many cards do you have in the suit and do you have entries in Dummy. If you need six tricks from this suit then you must cross back to you own hand and repeat the finesse until the K appears. However, with only one card in the suit, in hand, you finesse once and then play the A, followed by top cards until the K appears, on the most likely split, 4:2, this leaves you with 2 winners in Dummy but you will need an entry to access them. With two cards in the suit and a 3:2 split, you finesse twice and then take the A. With 3 cards in hand and a 3:1 split, when you finesse the first time and the K dose not appear you can be sure it is with W, so you finesse again and then play the A.

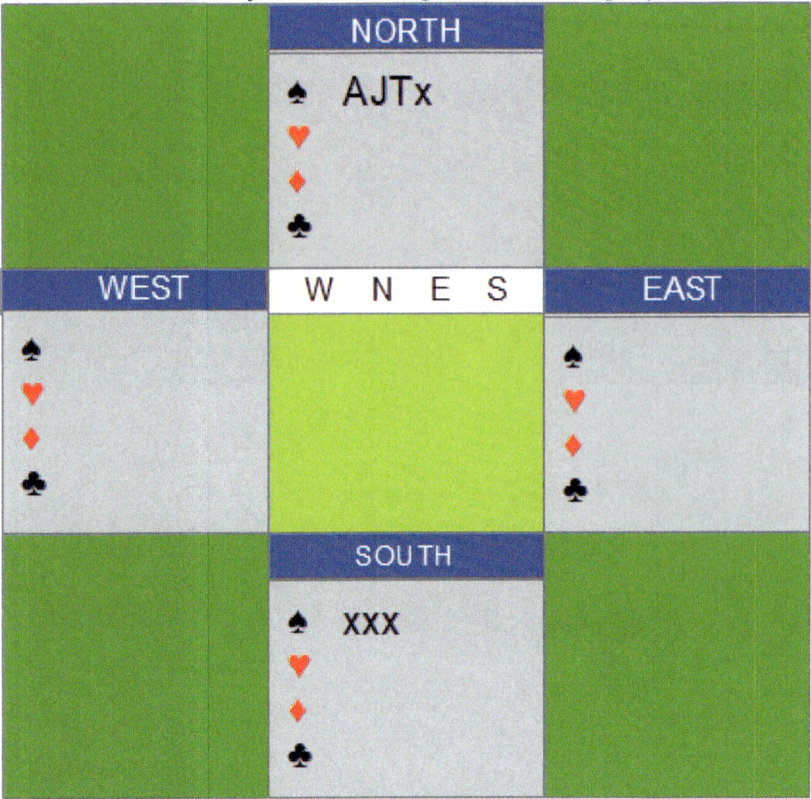

|  | NORTH ♠ AJTx ♥ ♦ ♣ |  |
|---|---|---|
| WEST ♠ ♥ ♦ ♣ | W N E S | EAST ♠ ♥ ♦ ♣ |
|  | SOUTH ♠ xxx ♥ ♦ ♣ |  |

When you need to establish winners in two suits, you may lose control and they take their winners in their long suit. This indicates the importance of establishing you suits as early as possible. Make your plan before playing the first card from Dummy. Sometimes the correct play to the first trick is the key to making the contract or an extra trick, so never rush to play from Dummy, think about your options first.

Above I have mentioned controls, this is a very important concept and particularly so in No Trumps. I shall always place declarer as South. Clearly, you are missing K & Q and need to make 3 tricks in this suit. The cards are most likely to be 4:2 in the suit. If K & Q are with East, you cannot succeed but neither will anyone else so you have to try the finesse. Either they have led this suit or you play low towards the AJT and we can consider all the possible outcomes. RHO plays low and you play the J or T according to taste, this is taken by the K from East. Now we have no idea where the Q is and they have the lead which they will use to try to establish their long suit. Declarer has the AK in their long suit so he has control of the suit. East plays low from their long suit and Declarer takes the trick, comes back to hand and leads low towards the AJx. There are now two possibilities, either West plays low or plays the Q. If West plays low you have to play the J and if East has the Q you lose the trick. If East takes the trick you need you second control to get back the lead. Whether you make 1, 2 or 3 tricks depends on the detail which I shall return to later as this example was purely about definition of and the need for controls.

How not to play a hand. I had a bad day at the office on the following hand:

|   | NORTH |   |
|---|---|---|
|   | ♠ QT75<br>♥ AQ3<br>♦ J72<br>♣ 873 |   |
| **WEST**<br>♠ AJ9832<br>♥ JT<br>♦ AT8<br>♣ 52 | W N E S<br>　　　　 1♦<br>1♠ 1NT 2♠ 3♣<br>3♠ 3NT P P<br>P | **EAST**<br>♠ K64<br>♥ K8654<br>♦ 64<br>♣ K64 |
|   | SOUTH<br>♠ -<br>♥ 972<br>♦ KQ953<br>♣ AQJT9 |   |

I was playing N and felt I had at least 1 stopper in ♠s after the 1♠ overcall, my partner clearly had at least 5:4 in ♦s and ♣ s and I assumed at least 16 points and 1 ♠ so I bid a risky 3NT which turned out to have only 21 HCPs but is makable if you play it correctly. Surprisingly, E led 5♥s which I took with the Q. Now my fatal error, after trick 1, I decided to establish the ♦ s and then return to finesse the ♣ s but neglected to note the ♣ s are self blocking and may need 2 finesses and the final play of the A to make 5 ♣ tricks. The defence was excellent, they held up the K♣s and the A♦s. Taking the third ♦ trick with the A and following with a ♥ to remove the entry in N. I could now take the first ♣ finesse but not the second as I am stuck in Dummy. At this stage play for as many tricks as you can get, 2 more ♦s, and a ♣ making 8 tricks.

The best approach after winning the first trick, finesse the ♣s and return a ♦. If E takes it he has set up the ♦s for you and you can return or be put back in to make the second ♣ finesse. This is an excellent example of the need to consider your entries, avoid blocking and estimate the splits. It is also an excellent example of hold up play and removing entries by the defenders, remember this for Chapter 9.

### 8.1.5 Techniques during play

Two more techniques that are important, playing hold up and losing into the correct hand. Lets say LHO leads a ♠ and you are strong in spades without the ace, your RHO takes the trick and leads the K of ♦. You are weak in ♦s but hold the ace and two low cards and from the likely splits you estimate your LHO has 3 ♦s so you let the RHO win the first two tricks in ♦s and take the 3rd with your ace. This is known as **hold-up**. At this stage you know RHO has two winners in ♦s maybe the 2 and the 3 and has become the **Danger Hand**. You are now in the position that you do not want to lose a trick to your RHO so you must finesse through RHO regardless of what all the other information, bidding and splits, tells you. You should make a safe cross to Dummy and lead to a tenace in your hand. Here is an example:

|       | NORTH           |       |
|-------|-----------------|-------|
|       | ♠ KJTx          |       |
|       | ♥ AQxx          |       |
|       | ♦ xx            |       |
|       | ♣ ?             |       |
| WEST  | W  N  E  S      | EAST  |
| ♠ Qxxx |                | ♠ Ax  |
| ♥ ?   |                 | ♥ ?   |
| ♦ xxx |                 | ♦ KQJxx |
| ♣ ?   |                 | ♣ ?   |
|       | SOUTH           |       |
|       | ♠ xxx           |       |
|       | ♥ xxx           |       |
|       | ♦ Axx           |       |
|       | ♣ AQJx          |       |

First trick goes 4♠, J♠, A♠, 2♠. The second trick goes K♦, 3♦, 5♦, 7♦. You have rightly broken the edict, "cover an honour with an honour" and you have held up the A♦ s. If you play the ace on the first round, E will surely make 4 ♦ tricks but if you wait until the third round, you can cross to Dummy via spades and finesse the K♣ s. If W has the K♣, he has no lead back to E that will give them 2 ♦ tricks. Note W must have the Q♠ as E used the A♠ to win the trick and W played low from 4 cards.

    Clearly, there are times when the only suit with a tenace leading to extra tricks is in Dummy and so you have to hope LHO has the honour you are trying to finesse otherwise RHO wins the trick and the contract goes off. Not all bad as everyone else in the room, in the same contract, will suffer the same fate. The important point is to play the hand in a way that maximise you chances of getting the most tricks for all the right reasons. Playing in this form you will make contracts when they are makable and go down when they are not. You might also find that a competing pair gets a good score, a top in Duplicate, because the defenders make a poor lead and give them an extra trick, there is nothing you can do about this except grin and bear in.

### 8.1.6 Finessing and Ducking

We have already seen a limited example of finessing in 8.1.4 &5 above, used to explain the concept of controls and hold up. I shall expand that example and give others as this is an important part of the play. I shall ignore the controls but have given all the cards in one suit that Declarer can't see.

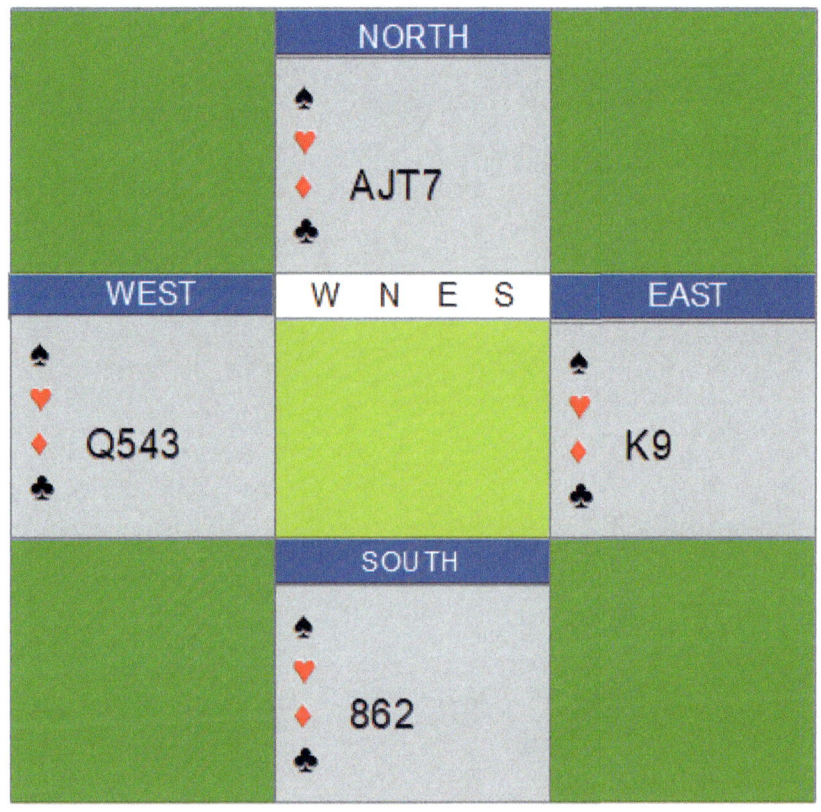

|  | NORTH<br>♠<br>♥<br>♦ AJT7<br>♣ |  |
|---|---|---|
| WEST<br>♠<br>♥<br>♦ Q543<br>♣ | W  N  E  S | EAST<br>♠<br>♥<br>♦ K9<br>♣ |
|  | SOUTH<br>♠<br>♥<br>♦ 862<br>♣ |  |

Now the declarer has to consider all the cards he can't see. They are KQ9543 and it important to look for KQ9 because they are potential winners and losers. Repeating the play: 2 is lead by S and 3 is played by W declarer puts up the T and E takes the trick with the K. S regains the lead and puts up the 6 and W plays the 4 followed by the J and 9. Now S knows W must have the Q and a low card as the 9 from E was unforced. Taking notice of significant cards being dropped tells you a great deal about where the remaining cards in the suit lie.

If on the second round W puts up the Q followed by the A from Dummy and the 9 from E again S knows the disposition of the remaining cards. In both of these cases Declarer makes 3 tricks and EW just 1.

Swap the cards around and Declarer makes just 1 trick instead of 3 but it is the same for every one else so don't be down hearted.

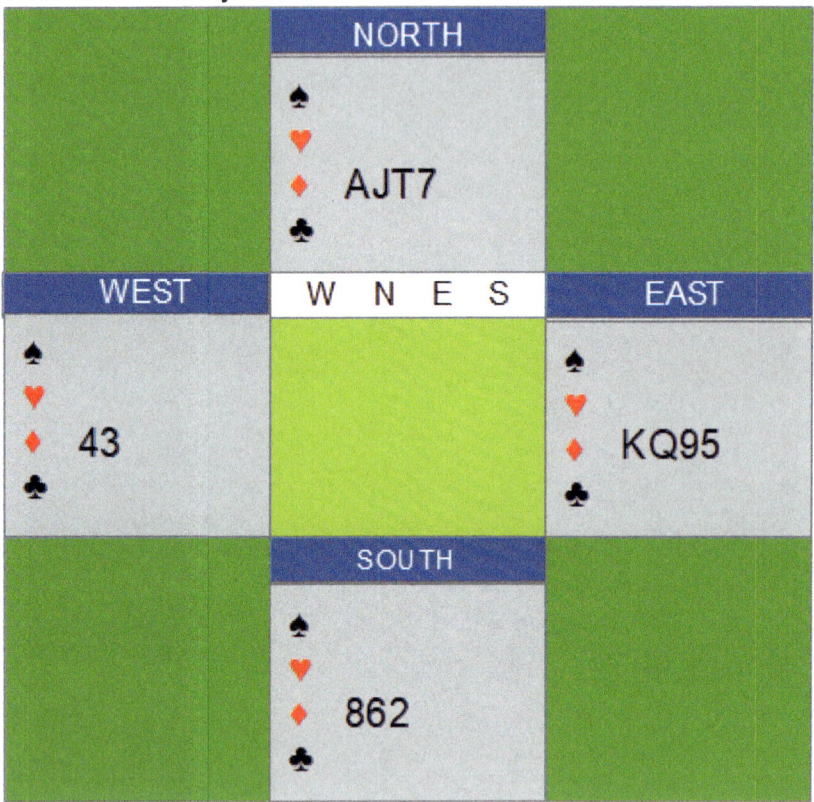

|  | NORTH ♠ ♥ ♦ AJT7 ♣ |  |
|---|---|---|
| WEST ♠ ♥ ♦ 43 ♣ | W  N  E  S | EAST ♠ ♥ ♦ KQ95 ♣ |
|  | SOUTH ♠ ♥ ♦ 862 ♣ |  |

The important point to take away is that you must enumerate all the cards outstanding and watch the "small" cards played by the opponent not competing for the trick.

Returning to our example in 8.1.4 with all cards in the suit showing

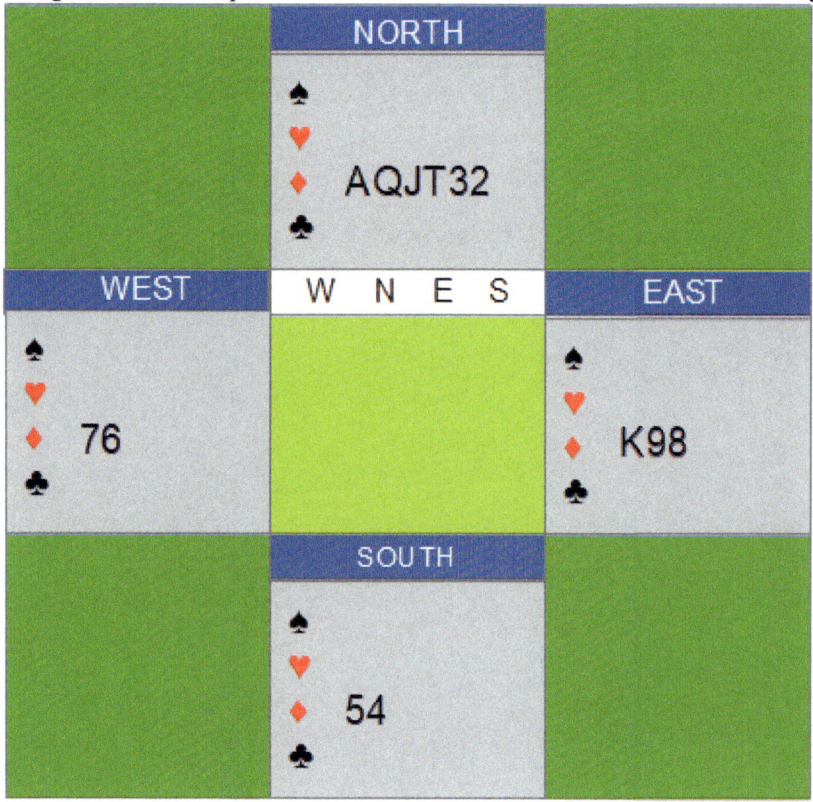

```
                    NORTH
                    ♠
                    ♥
                    ♦ AQJT32
                    ♣
      WEST      W  N  E  S     EAST
      ♠                         ♠
      ♥                         ♥
      ♦ 76                      ♦ K98
      ♣                         ♣
                    SOUTH
                    ♠
                    ♥
                    ♦ 54
                    ♣
```

Declarer knows the K9876 are with the defenders. On the first finesse, the play is 4, 6, Q, 8 and the Declarer stops to think about each card played. E did not start with K singleton or K doubleton, on the latter E would play the K on the first round because he could lose it if the A is played next. When declarer crosses to his own hand and plays the 5 and this is followed by the 7 he confidently plays the J but what will E do? E has to play the K for the same reason as starting with a doubleton. Declarer can only cash his three winners if he has an entry in Dummy. In NT it is important to set up this suit as early as possible in the play.

**Watch for significant cards being dropped.**

Now we can consider how to play a poor suit. East leads low in a new suit, so it is likely to be 4 cards, here is the distribution:

|        | NORTH      |        |
|--------|------------|--------|
|        | ♠          |        |
|        | ♥          |        |
|        | ♦          |        |
|        | ♣ 762      |        |
| WEST   | W N E S    | EAST   |
| ♠      |            | ♠      |
| ♥      |            | ♥      |
| ♦      |            | ♦      |
| ♣ A94  |            | ♣ QJT5 |
|        | SOUTH      |        |
|        | ♠          |        |
|        | ♥          |        |
|        | ♦          |        |
|        | ♣ K83      |        |

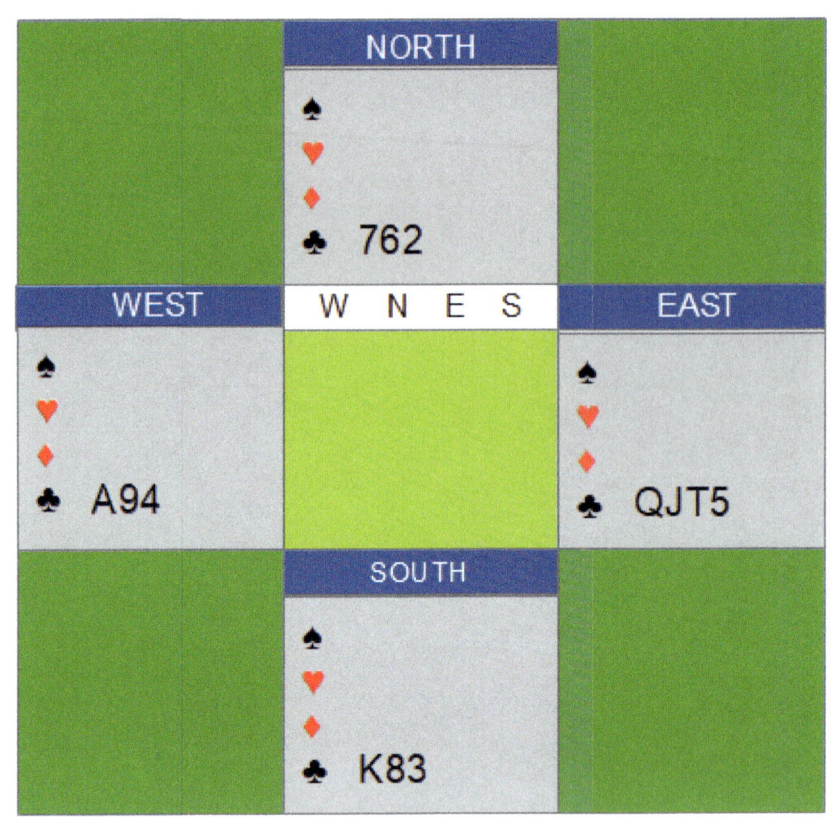

E leads the 5 and Declarer plays the 3, as he has 876 and W may play the 9 and N plays the 2. W can play the A or the 4 but it is a dilemma, if he plays the A, he establishes the K as a winner. If he plays the 4, S wins with the K and gains 1 trick in the suit. If S was unwise enough to play the K on the first trick, EW win 4 tricks in the suit. Of course, if W returns lead to E via a different suit and E plays high from this suit EW make four tricks provided they can return lead to E again. In general it is best to play low from Kxx on the first round. This is essentially a hold up and note again, do not cover an honour with an honour when RHO has a sequence.

### 8.1.7 Establishing a long suit

Consider this suit:

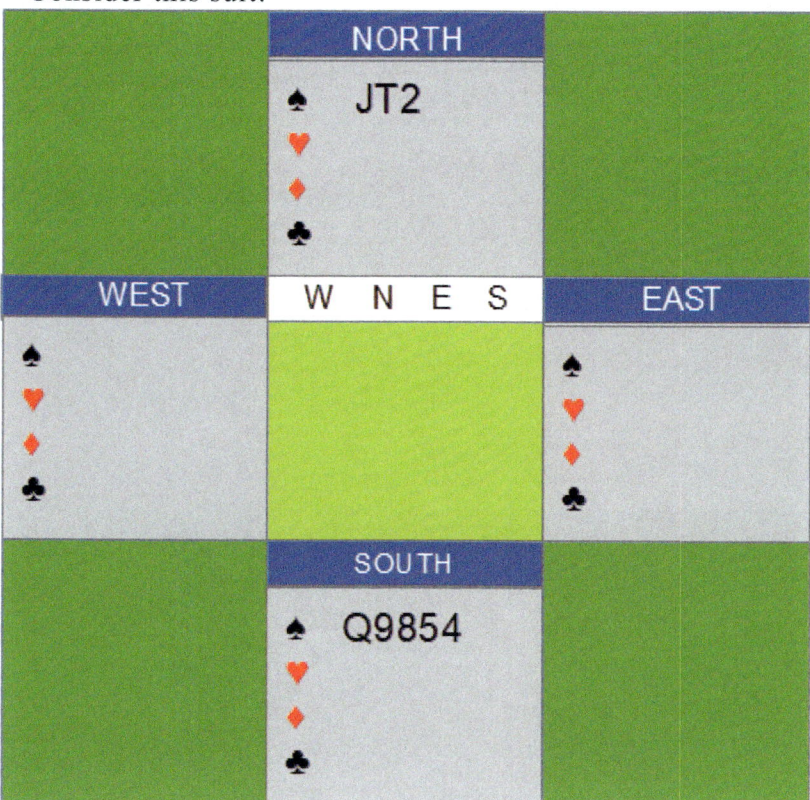

|  | NORTH ♠ JT2 |  |
|---|---|---|
| WEST ♠ | W N E S | EAST ♠ |
|  | SOUTH ♠ Q9854 |  |

You want to make 3 tricks in the suit so you play the 4 towards the J and lose to the K in E. At your next chance you play the 5 towards Dummy or the T from Dummy. In both cases you play the T and lose to the A. You now have three winners in your hand.

Another long suit example:

**NORTH**
♠
♥ Q32
♦
♣

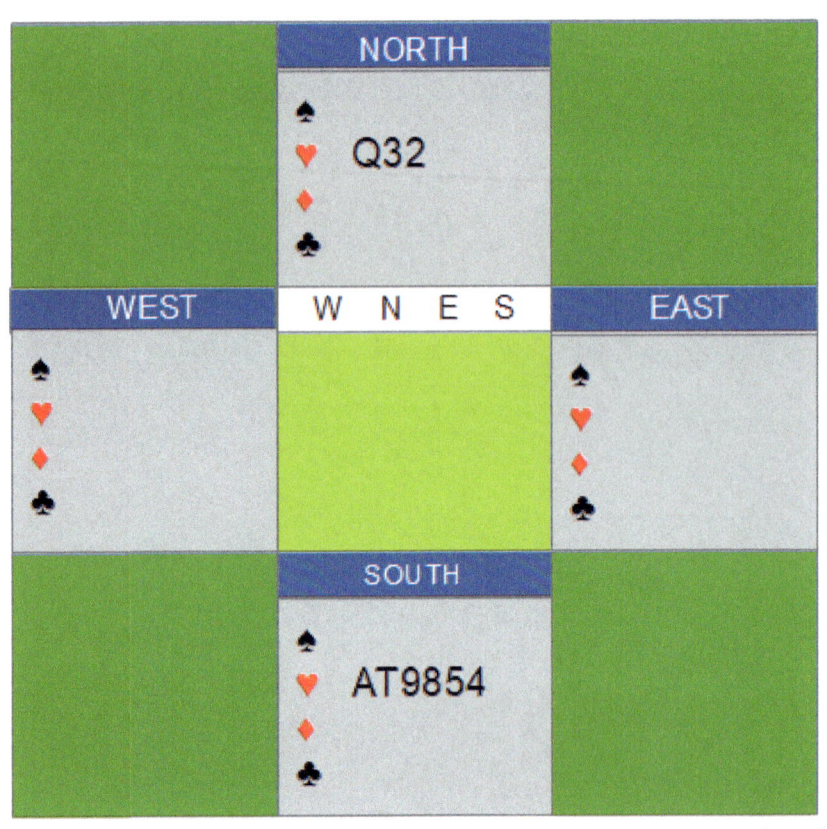

**WEST**
♠
♥
♦
♣

**EAST**
♠
♥
♦
♣

**SOUTH**
♠
♥ AT9854
♦
♣

This does not look promising but it is a 9 cards suit. You play the A followed by low ♥ towards the Q: but you should note the cards played by the opposition. If W plays the J, it is almost certain that E has K76 and you put up the Q. Now or later E takes their 1 trick in this suit. The worst case is E has KJ76 and they take 2 tricks unless you know from the bidding that KJ is likely to be with E, in which case you start by finessing E towards the AT and they make 1 trick provided you have the necessary entries to Dummy.

### 8.1.8 Using the Auction

Lets look at the example 8.1.5 again.

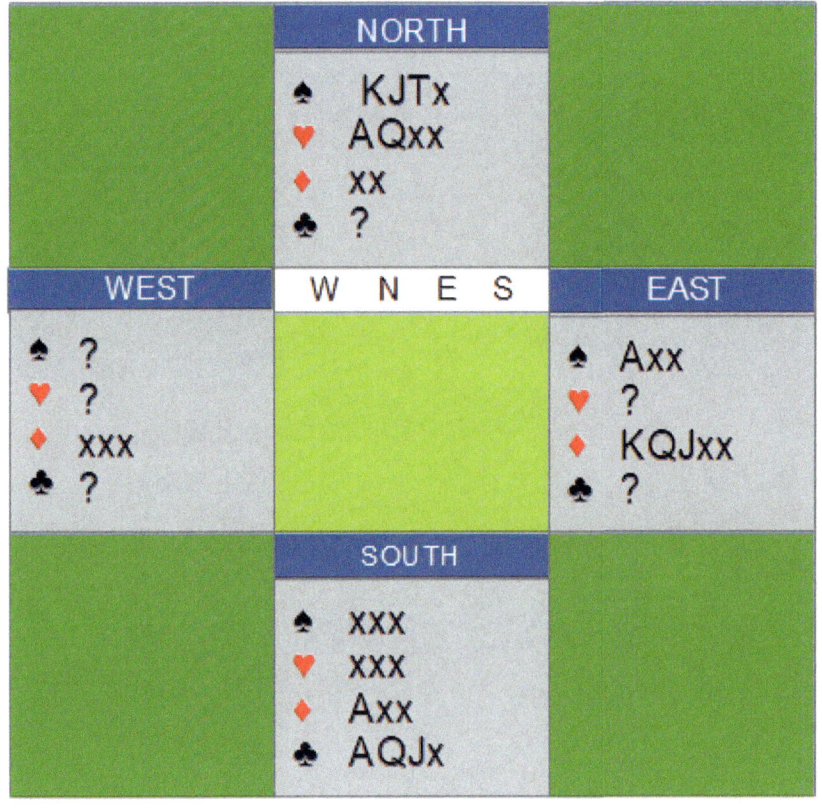

|  | NORTH |  |
|---|---|---|
|  | ♠ KJTx<br>♥ AQxx<br>♦ xx<br>♣ ? |  |
| WEST | | EAST |
| ♠ ?<br>♥ ?<br>♦ xxx<br>♣ ? | | ♠ Axx<br>♥ ?<br>♦ KQJxx<br>♣ ? |
|  | SOUTH |  |
|  | ♠ xxx<br>♥ xxx<br>♦ Axx<br>♣ AQJx |  |

This time NS are in 3NT with S as declarer and E made an overcall described as intermediate with at least 5♦s. W will play a ♦ and declarer knows that E has 12 HCPs and W has no more than 3. S cannot get back to N without losing a trick and E making 4♦ tricks. He may lose the K♥ and A♠ for 2 off. This often happens when one hand has most of the outstanding points. The only chance of making the contract is if W has the K♥ and the lower cards enable S to make 4♥ s, 4♣ s and 1 ♦ . One could criticise S for bidding 3NT with only one stop after the 2♦ bid by E.

85

### 8.1.9 Unblocking during play.

You may be in a position to take a trick in hand or in Dummy but it can be fatal to take it in the wrong one, here is a simple example:

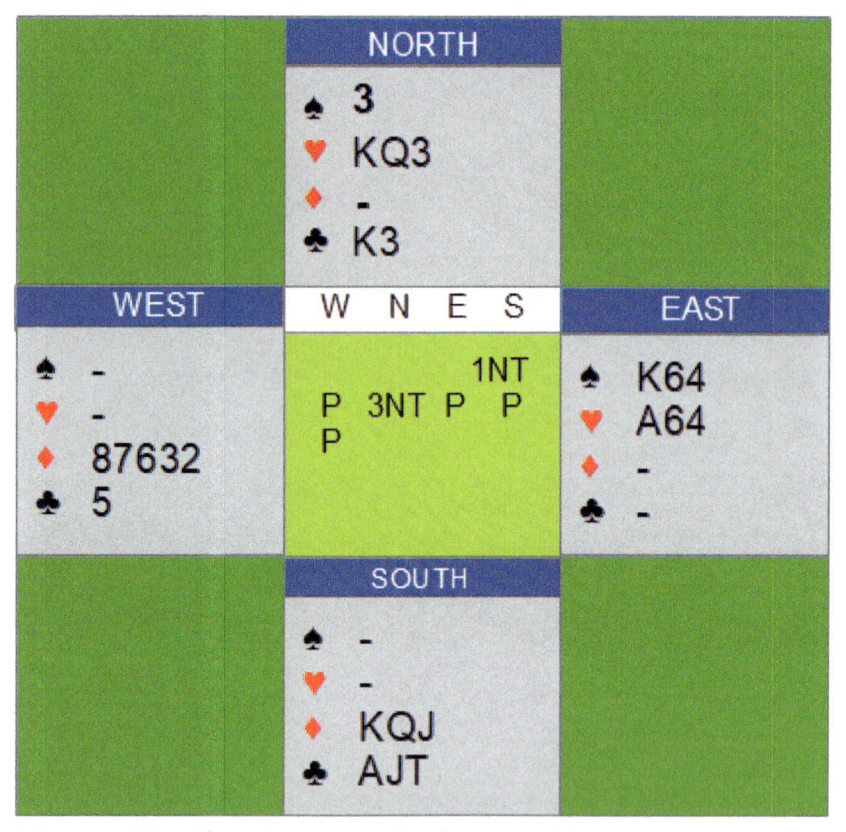

|  | NORTH<br>♠ 3<br>♥ KQ3<br>♦ -<br>♣ K3 |  |
|---|---|---|
| WEST<br>♠ -<br>♥ -<br>♦ 87632<br>♣ 5 | W N E S<br>　　　　1NT<br>P 3NT P P<br>P | EAST<br>♠ K64<br>♥ A64<br>♦ -<br>♣ - |
|  | SOUTH<br>♠ -<br>♥ -<br>♦ KQJ<br>♣ AJT |  |

Play has progressed and W is on lead, you still need six tricks to make the contract. W leads the 5♣s and you sloppily play the 3♣, second hand plays low, followed by the A♣s. Now if you play the clubs, the next club lands you in Dummy and you lose at least 1 trick. If you play the K and cover it with the A, you win the 6 final tricks. This is known as **unblocking** and is a standard tactic that may occur in more complicated forms.

## 8.2 Declarer play in a suit.

Many of the techniques used in NT contracts can be used when playing in a suit contract but the thinking is different from the outset.

When a suit contract has been bid, the LHO plays a card and the Dummy goes down on the table, now the thinking begins. You repeat everything laid out in 8.1.1 to 8.1.3. Now, consider your own hand with Dummy's hand and count how many tricks you might lose. Count the number of tricks you would win by drawing the trumps and playing you top card and finally the surplus trumps, hopefully but not necessarily as a cross ruff. Can you make enough tricks for the contract, if not can you make extra tricks directly, think about the seven possible approaches and particularly taking a short side ruff, establishing a long suit or taking a finesse. Remember in duplicate it is important to make over tricks even at the risk of going off where as in Teams making the contract is paramount where over tricks are a small bonus, see Section 8.3.

### 8.2.1 Short side ruff.

One source of extra tricks is to ruff in the short side, when the trumps are unevenly split, before drawing trumps. To do this without getting over ruffed you need to estimate the split and do it only until one of you opponents is likely to run out. S is in a ♠ contract and it is the second trick and S is on lead, the ♥ split is likely to be 6:4 but 8:2, 7:3 and 5:5 are not a problem so lead A♥ s followed by the 9 and ruff with the 2♠ s in Dummy .

```
              NORTH
              ♠ 762
              ♥ 8
              ♦
              ♣
  WEST      W N E S      EAST
  ♠                        ♠
  ♥                        ♥
  ♦                        ♦
  ♣                        ♣
              SOUTH
              ♠ AKQ83
              ♥ A9
              ♦
              ♣
```

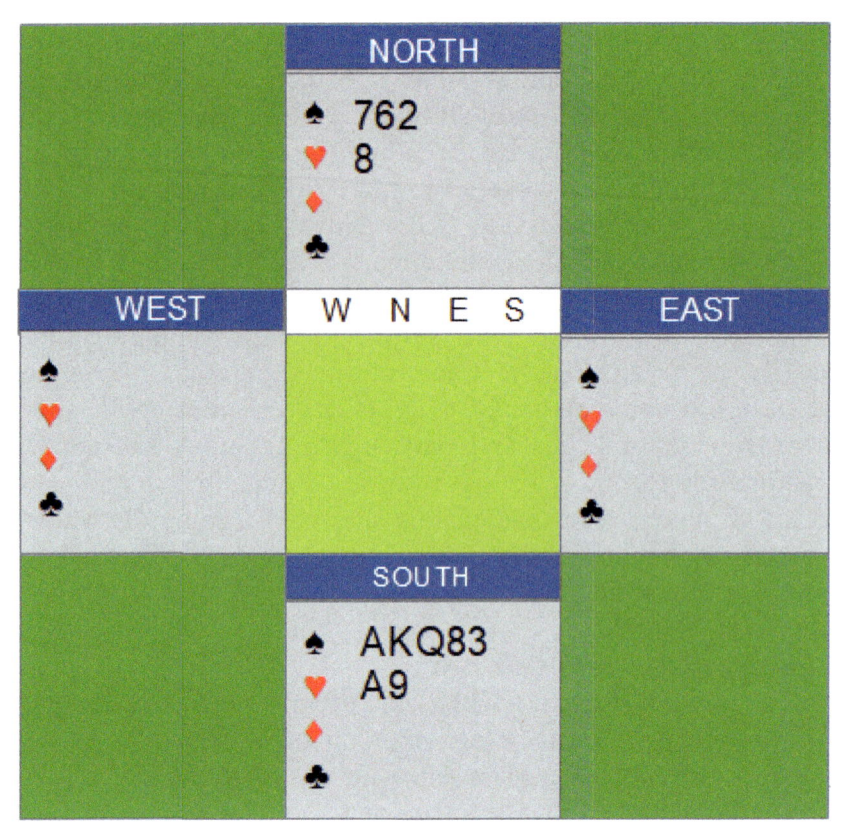

If you drew the trumps first you would make 1 less trick.

### 8.2.2 The Cross Ruff

A number of suit hands possess a sufficient number of trumps and shortages in other suits so you can make extra tricks. Here is an example:

|       | NORTH       |       |
|-------|-------------|-------|
|       | ♠ T3        |       |
|       | ♥ JT83      |       |
|       | ♦ AKxxx     |       |
|       | ♣ xx        |       |

| WEST | W | N | E | S | EAST |
|------|---|---|---|---|------|
| ♠    |   |   |   | 1♠ | ♠   |
| ♥    | P | 2♦ | P | 3♠ | ♥  |
| ♦    | P | 4♠ | P | P  | ♦  |
| ♣    | P |    |   |    | ♣  |

|       | SOUTH       |
|-------|-------------|
|       | ♠ AKJ842    |
|       | ♥ A9        |
|       | ♦ x         |
|       | ♣ AKxx      |

W leads a low ♥. S decides the ♦s and ♣s and ♥s will split 4:3 and the ♠s 3:2. There are 13 HCPs outstanding and they are likely to split 6:7 in the defenders hands. The play may progress as follows: trick 1, 2♥ 3♥ K♥ A♥, trick 2 and 3 A and K ♣s from S, all follow and no honour appears from W or E, trick 4 low ♣ from S ruffed low in N tricks 5 and 6 A&K♦ from N, all follow but S discards the 9♥, trick 7 low ♦, E follows, S plays the 8 ♠s and W follows, they were 4:3 in ♦s. Trick 8 S plays a low club to the T♠s and it holds, again the split is 4:3, trick 9 S plays a ♥ from Dummy and ruffs it as the split is 4:3. S now takes 2 round of trumps and will lose one on a 3:2 split when the Q is in the 3 card hand. With a 4:1 split in trumps you still make 11 tricks but in a 5:0 probably only 10. Taking out the trumps first you will only make 10 tricks on a most probable split, half the time, on all other splits the contract goes off.

### 8.2.3 Throw a loser on a winner or a loser.

Another technique is to throw away losers in one hand on winners in the other by this you can create ruffs in the opposite hand. You are in 4♠s having lost one trick, regained the lead in S and hold the remaining ♠s:

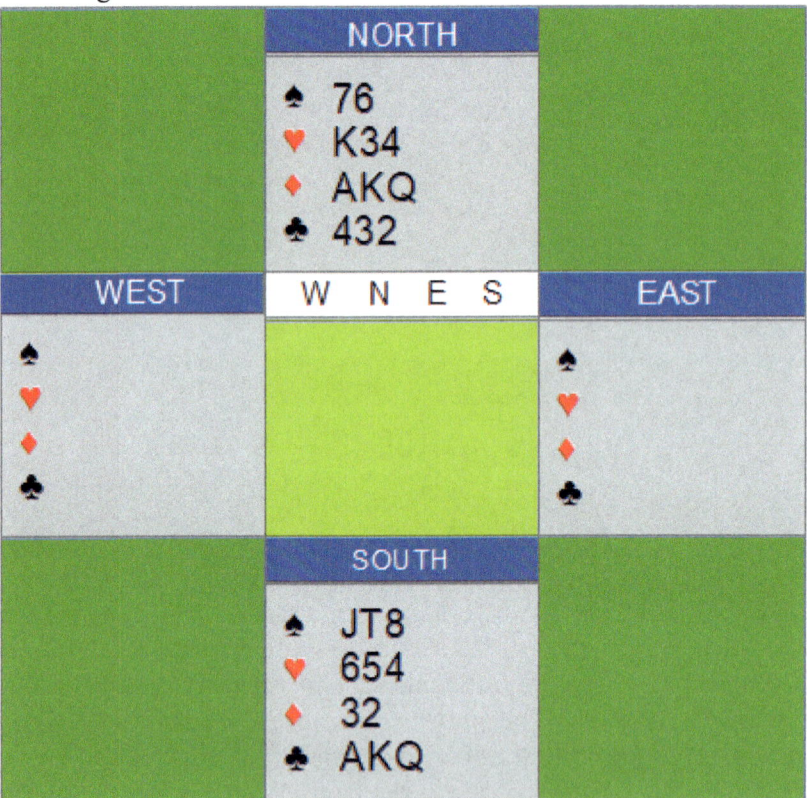

|  | NORTH | |
|---|---|---|
|  | ♠ 76 <br> ♥ K34 <br> ♦ AKQ <br> ♣ 432 | |
| WEST <br> ♠ <br> ♥ <br> ♦ <br> ♣ | W  N  E  S | EAST <br> ♠ <br> ♥ <br> ♦ <br> ♣ |
|  | SOUTH <br> ♠ JT8 <br> ♥ 654 <br> ♦ 32 <br> ♣ AKQ | |

It is tempting to play low to the K♥s with a 50:50 chance of winning the trick but the better play is to cross to the A♦s and play the K&Q discarding a ♥ from your hand on the Q♦s. You can now return to your hand via a ♣ and now try the 50:50 chance on the K♥s. This guarantees the contract, by discarding a loser, and may make an over trick if the K♥s holds. Playing to the K first may give them three tricks but discarding a ♥ first cuts it to two.

You can also throw a loser on a loser. Take this example:

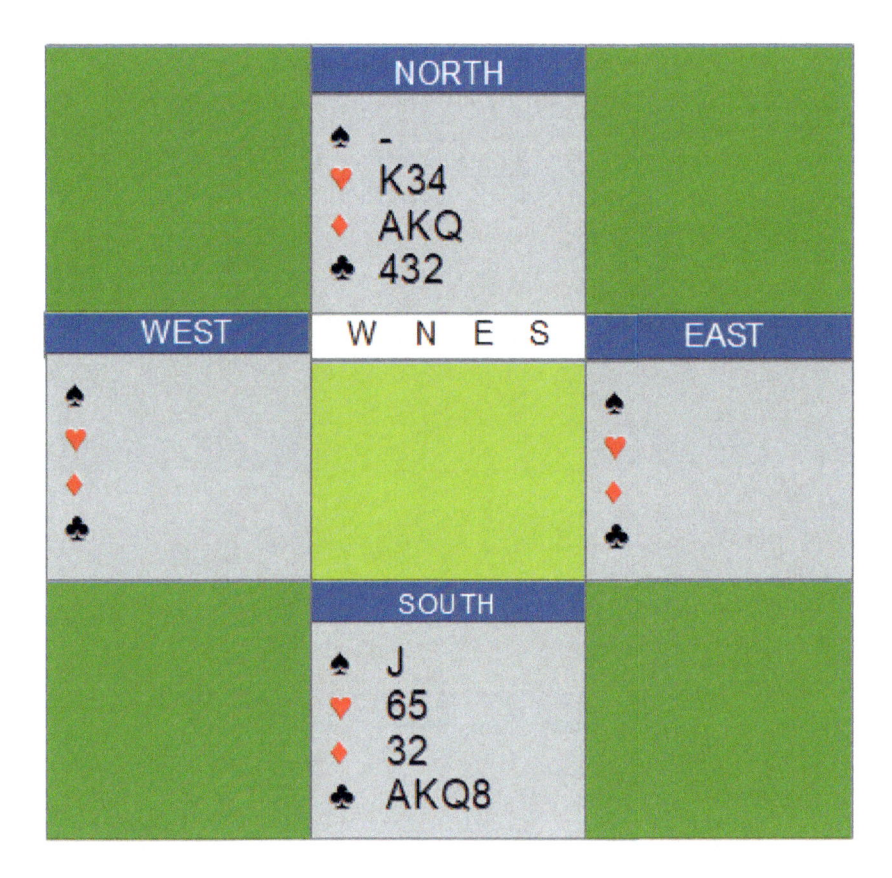

```
           NORTH
         ♠  -
         ♥  K34
         ♦  AKQ
         ♣  432

WEST     W  N  E  S    EAST
♠                      ♠
♥                      ♥
♦                      ♦
♣                      ♣

           SOUTH
         ♠  J
         ♥  65
         ♦  32
         ♣  AKQ8
```

As above you play the AKQ♣ and several things can happen: if they are 3:3, you make the 8♣ and discard a ♥ ; if W shows out (discards a card from a different suit), you play the 8♣ s and discard a ♥ losing the trick into E, the K must make wherever the A is.

In a suit where you have unavoidable losers it is better to lose a trick or two early on and collect winners with small cards later on. This is equally applicable to NT contracts.

### 8.2.4 Finessing in a suit contract

Lets return to my example in 8.1.6. which was how to play this in a NT contract.

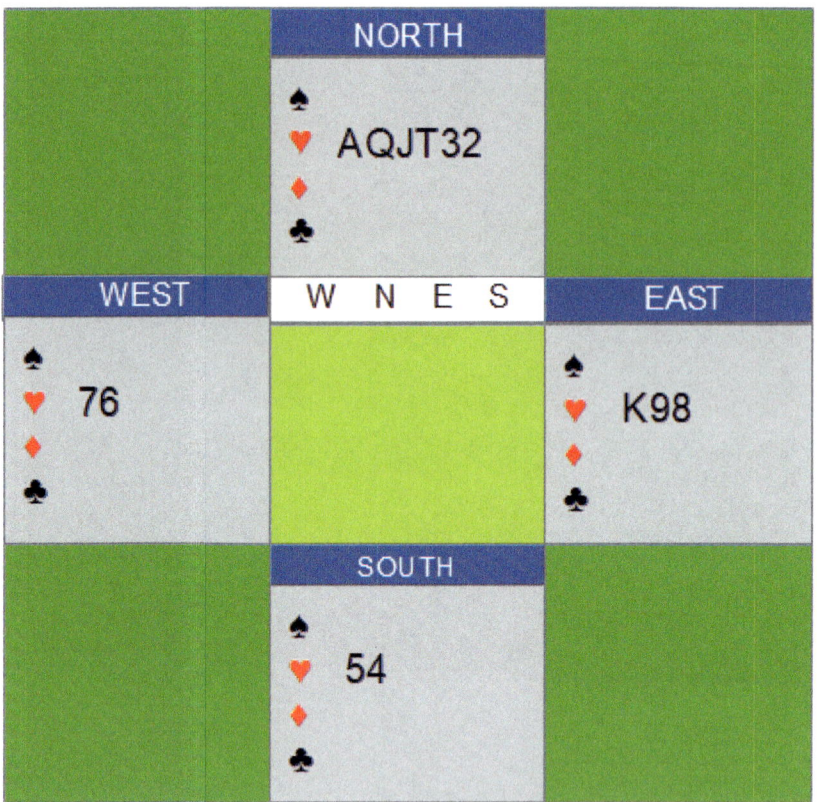

```
                NORTH
                ♠
                ♥ AQJT32
                ♦
                ♣

WEST            W  N  E  S            EAST
♠                                     ♠
♥ 76                                  ♥ K98
♦                                     ♦
♣                                     ♣

                SOUTH
                ♠
                ♥ 54
                ♦
                ♣
```

Now the play changes a little, if the first finesse holds because E does not play his K. Declarer plays the A and E plays the 9 and W the 6. Declarer does not need to know where the K is as he can ruff it on the next round of this suit. This requires 1 entry in Dummy to cash the rest of the suit. When you draw trumps and when you take the finesse become strategic decisions in your game plan, in a suit contract.

### 8.2.5 Establishing a long suit

Consider this suit:

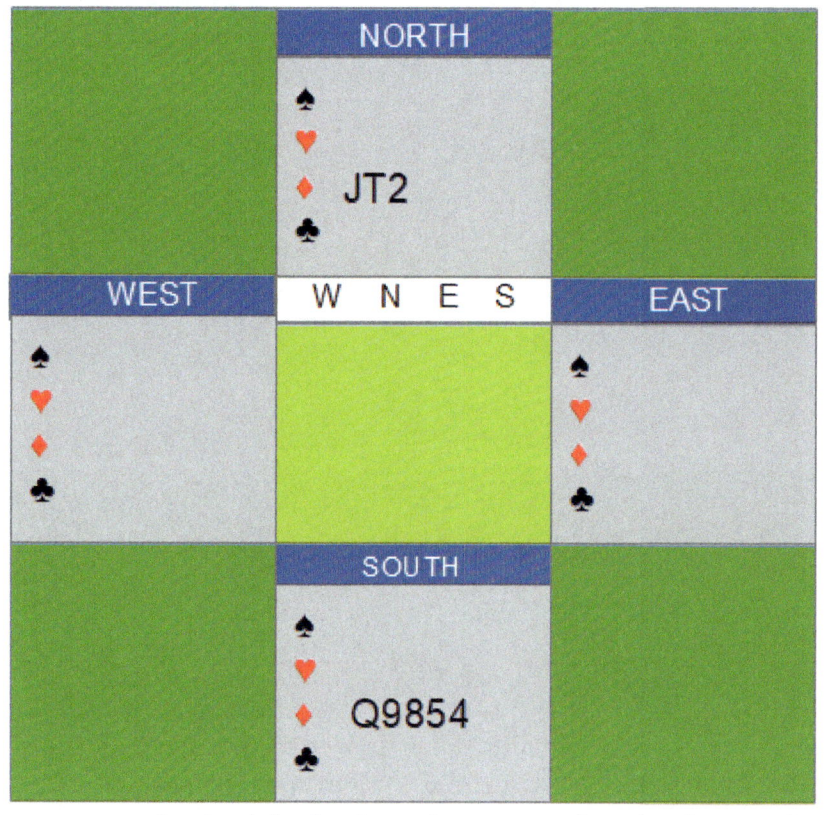

|  | NORTH |  |
|---|---|---|
|  | ♦ JT2 |  |
| WEST | W N E S | EAST |
|  | SOUTH |  |
|  | ♦ Q9854 |  |

You want to make 3 tricks in the suit so you play the 4 towards the J and lose to the K in E. At your next chance you play the 5 towards Dummy or the T from Dummy. In both cases you play the T and lose to the A. You now have three winners in your hand **provided you have drawn trumps before attacking this suit.**

Another long suit example:

```
            NORTH
             ♠
             ♥
             ♦
             ♣ Q32

WEST        W  N  E  S        EAST
 ♠                             ♠
 ♥                             ♥
 ♦                             ♦
 ♣                             ♣

            SOUTH
             ♠
             ♥
             ♦
             ♣ AT9854
```

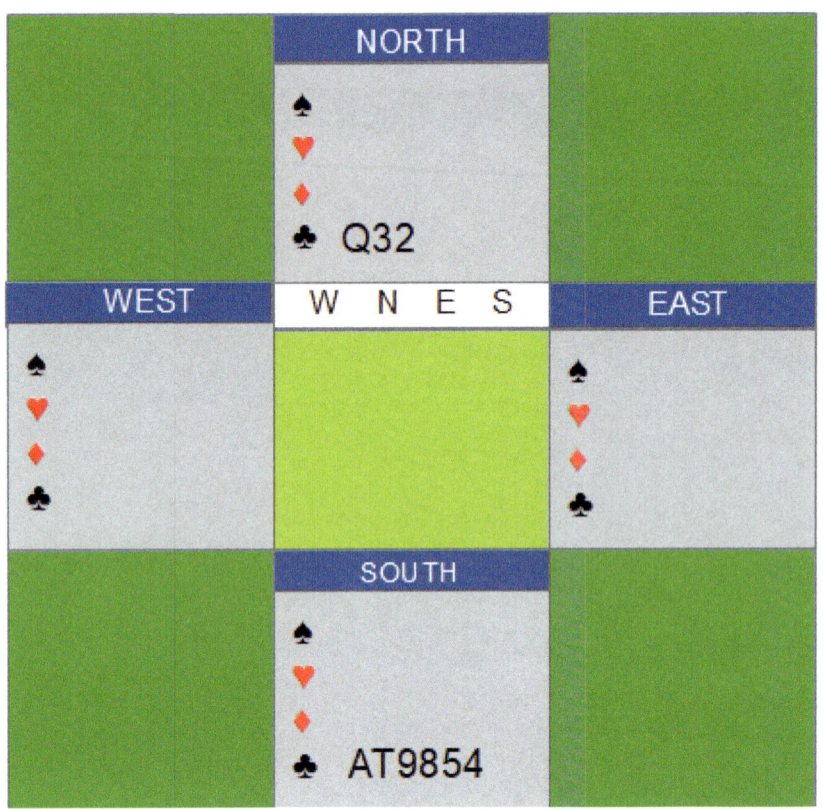

This does not look promising but it is a 9 cards suit. You play the A followed by the low towards the Q: but you should note the cards played by the opposition. If W plays the J on the first trick, it is almost certain that E has K76 and you put up the Q. Now or later E takes their 1 trick in this suit. The worst case is E has KJ76 and they take 2 tricks unless you know from the bidding that KJ is likely to be with E, in which case you start finessing E towards the AT and they make 1 trick. You must take out trumps before you start on this suit as it may only go one round before they ruff

## 8.3 Teams versus Duplicate
This is so important it is worth repeating Section 5.1, so here is a copy :
### 8.3.1 Scoring in Duplicate and Teams

It is assumed the reader is familiar with the scoring of a contract based upon the outcome: e.g.

4♥ Vulnerable 1 off, 100 points
4♠ non-vulnerable making, 420 points
3♦ X non-vulnerable making 11, 670 points
1NT either vulnerability making, 90 points

The scores are the same whether you are playing Duplicate or Teams however the implications are different.

In Duplicate let us consider a match where there are 4 tables and 6 rounds of 4 boards each. Each boards is played 4 times and you play 6 rounds against 6 other pairs, you don't play against 1 pair and which one depends upon where you start. This can be played as a Wigan ¾ Howell movement and the movement cards are given in Appendix D. After playing all 24 boards you get a % score and a rank position based upon your %. Now each pair plays 24 boards and if they made one more trick than everyone else on each board they would gain 100% so each board is worth 4 1/6 %. Dropping the fraction, if you make a mess of the bidding or play one board badly you lose 2% relative to the mean. Consequently, the score on one board will not significantly affect your match score. A typical range of scores for 24 boards is 30 to 70 % because a number of boards will always result in the same contract making the same number of tricks and everyone gets 2%. So success is achieved by being in the right contract and making one more trick than anyone else whether Declarer or Defender. Defending well in a part score or game contract making one extra trick is just as important as making an extra trick in a small slam.

Scoring in Teams is different. Usually two teams of four play 24 boards. In the first half, Team A NS plays 12 boards against Team B pair a and at the same time, Team A EW plays the same 12 boards against Team B pair b. After half time refreshments, Team A NS plays against Team B pair b and Team A pair EW plays Team B pair a for a further 12 boards. In this way each pair plays 24 boards and plays 12 against each pair of the opposing team.

Here is an example of scoring in a Team match on the first 4 boards:
The first four boards

| Hand No. | VUL | Versus TEAM or PAIR No. | CONTRACT | BY | TRICKS | SCORE PLUS | SCORE MINUS | MATCH POINTS A | MATCH POINTS B |
|---|---|---|---|---|---|---|---|---|---|
| 1/ | — | A NS | 4H | N | 10 | 420 | | 0 | |
| 2/ | NS | A NS | 6S | N | 12 | 1430 | | 13 | |
| 3/ | EW | A NS | 2H | E | 8 | | 110 | 0 | |
| 4/ | ALL | A NS | 3H | N | 10 | 170 | | 6 | |
| 5/ | NS | | | | | | | | |

| Hand No. | VUL | Versus TEAM or PAIR No. | CONTRACT | BY | TRICKS | SCORE PLUS | SCORE MINUS | MATCH POINTS | |
|---|---|---|---|---|---|---|---|---|---|
| 1/ | — | A EW | 4H | N | 10 | | 420 | | |
| 2/ | NS | A EW | 4S | N | 12 | | 680 | | |
| 3/ | EW | A EW | 2S | N | 6 | 100 | | | |
| 4/ | ALL | A EW | 4H | N | 10 | | 620 | | |
| 5/ | NS | | | | | | | | |

Match points in IMPS.

```
IMP    0 -  10 = 0 IMP      320 -  360 = 8 IMP      1300 - 1490 = 16 IMP
      20 -  40 = 1 IMP      370 -  420 = 9 IMP      1500 - 1740 = 17 IMP
      50 -  80 = 2 IMP      430 -  490 =10 IMP      1750 - 1990 = 18 IMP
      90 - 120 = 3 IMP      500 -  590 =11 IMP      2000 - 2240 = 19 IMP
     130 - 160 = 4 IMP      600 -  740 =12 IMP      2250 - 2490 = 20 IMP
     170 - 210 = 5 IMP      750 -  890 =13 IMP      2500 - 2990 = 21 IMP
     220 - 260 = 6 IMP      900 - 1090 =14 IMP      3000 - 3490 = 22 IMP
     270 - 310 = 7 IMP     1100 - 1290 =15 IMP      3500 - 3990 = 23 IMP
                                                    4000 and up = 24 IMP
```

The first score card belongs to Team A NS and the second is from Team A EW, Team B will have mirror images of these two cards, I have chosen the stationary team to illustrate some important points, pun intended. On board 1 the contract was 4♥ s played by North at each table and both made 10 tricks. The net score is found by adding the two cards 420 + (-420) = 0 and the IMP table gives 0 so enter 0 match points for Team A. On board 2, N plays in 6♠ s making 12 tricks whereas at Table 2 N plays in 4♠ s making 12 tricks. This gives a net score of 750 to Team A and the match point table gives 13 IMPs. Following the same process the IMPs for board 3 are 0 and board 4 are -6, i.e 6 for Team B. The overall score is found by adding up the match points on all 24 boards, usually carried out at half time and full time. A typical score would be 56:47 for A:B indicating A won the match by 9 Match Points.

Now we can consider the importance of bidding a slam if it is possible or likely to make rather than settling for game. Equally, not bidding game when it is possible to make is a disaster. In the example above Team A bid and made a slam whilst Team B bid game and made 12 tricks. This gave Team A 13 IMPs and was enough to turn defeat to victory. One bad board can lose you the whole match at Teams whilst at Duplicate it might reduce your rank by one place. This leads to the idea of bidding game or a slam on one point less than you would do in Duplicate.

### *Always bid a marginal game or Slam*

Consider the bids at the beginning of this section made at Teams:
3♦ X making 11 670 points versus 3♦ making 11 150 points This gives a net score of 520 points and results in 11 IMPS to the side that **did not** **double**. Consider the auction:

1♠ P 3♠ P 4♦ P 4♥ P 6♠ X(P) P P

You hold the A♠ s and the AK of ♦ s so Double. No! Why not, the bidding shows declarer has first round control of ♦ s, 4♦ Cue bid, you know this must be a void so you are unlikely to make either of your ♦ honours.

*In Teams never double a contract unless you are sure to take it off.*

### 8.3.2 Examples of play in Duplicate and Teams.

In Teams the imperative is to make your contract whereas in Duplicate the imperative is to make an overtrick.

For example, you are down to AQ♥ in Dummy, you are on lead with only 2 low ♥s, Kx♥ are still out and you have no idea where they are. You also need one trick to make the contract. You play your heart toward Dummy and inspect the card played by your RHO. If a ♥ is played, in Teams you play the A♥ but in Duplicate you play the Q♥ as you have about a 50:50 chance of making an extra trick. If the RHO does not play a ♥ then, of course, you play the A♥ in Teams and Duplicate.

### 8.4 Plays for the expert.*

The next three sections may be skipped by the Newcomer. I have only once knowingly executed any of these techniques; they are here for completeness and so that you are not left in the dark when someone talks about how they carried one out but more often, pretentiously, about how they should have used one of them with 20:20 hindsight.

### 8.4.1 Squeeze plays

The essence of the squeeze play {13} is to set up one of your opponents so they have the choice between discards and which ever they chose, you can then discard a losing card and keep a winning card. The concept is easy enough but the execution requires that you track every card played and their significance. Beyond the capabilities of most players including myself.

Taking a simple example from Reese {13}

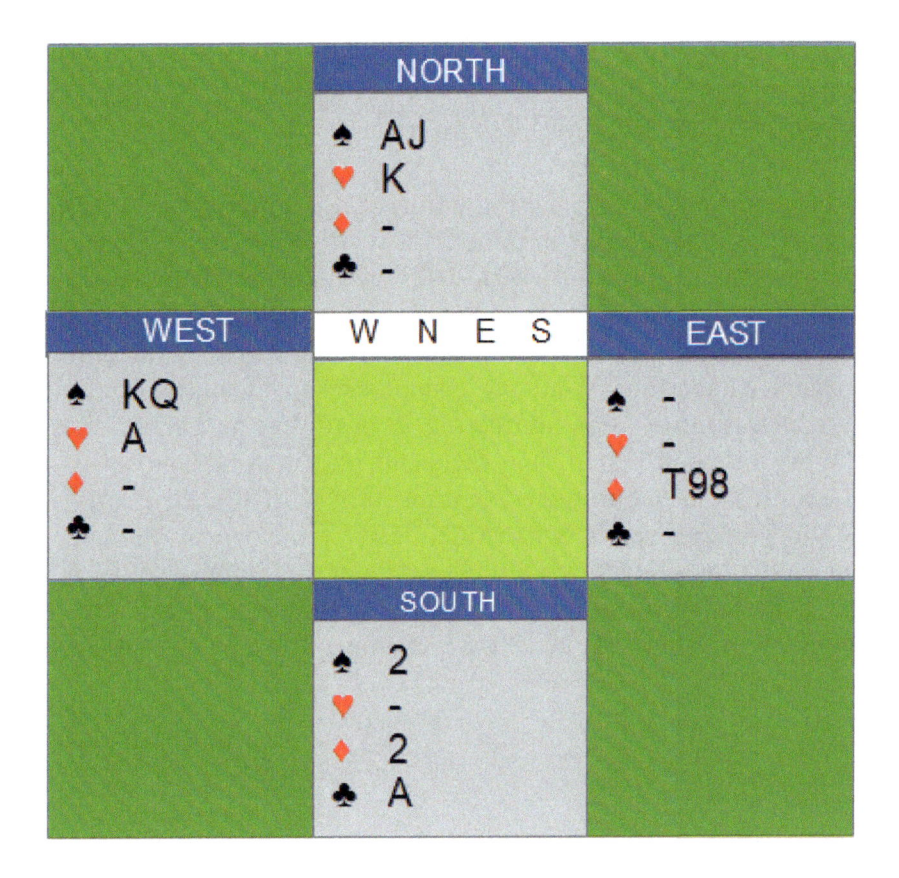

|  | NORTH | |
|---|---|---|
|  | ♠ AJ<br>♥ K<br>♦ -<br>♣ - |  |
| WEST | W N E S | EAST |
| ♠ KQ<br>♥ A<br>♦ -<br>♣ - |  | ♠ -<br>♥ -<br>♦ T98<br>♣ - |
|  | SOUTH |  |
|  | ♠ 2<br>♥ -<br>♦ 2<br>♣ A |  |

S is on lead and plays A♣s, now W has to discard a winner. If he discards the K or Q of ♠s, you discard the K♥s from Dummy and the A&J♠s become winners. If W discards the A♥s, you discard the J♠s from Dummy and the A♠s and the K♥s become winners. So whatever W does you win the three final tricks. **Timing**, you must arrive at this point knowing where the **Threat Cards** (KQ♠s & A♥s) are, have a **Squeeze Card** (A♣s) and have **Communication** (2♠s) with Dummy. This also assumes that the contract is in NT or ♣s. I have only once managed to be in this position knowingly.

A simpler view is when you have a long suit that are all winners and possible losers in other suits, as above, is to play the long suit and carefully watch the discards of your opponents, remembering any information such as the lead, cards played and bidding that will pin point where the crucial cards are. You can then make a rational end play that will maximise your chances of making the most tricks.

### 8.4.2 Strip and Throw-In

Here again you have an awkward ending and you need to maximise your tricks to make the contract. Something one always tries to do is avoid giving your opponents a ruff and discard. So you try to **strip** away their opportunities to do this and then give them the lead (**throw-in**) so they have to lead to your awkward suit. This ties up with a more general principle of leaving a difficult suit to your opponents, don't try to establish it yourself. I shall use an example from Klinger {5} to illustrate this. It is interesting to note that he gives 8 examples and the are all Small Slam contracts but only a small subset of Small Slams require this technique. Combine this with the rarity of bidding Slams and you can see it is marginal activity but worth knowing of its existence. Bridge players are a wide range of characters, some of whom love to mention all these complex tactics without the slightest clue how they work, most amusing. Here is an example from {5}:

```
                NORTH
              ♠ 8
              ♥ J984
              ♦ 876
              ♣ QJT32
   WEST        W N E S        EAST
♠ JT972                     ♠ AK43
♥ AK5                       ♥ 7632
♦ AKQ                       ♦ JT2
♣ AK                        ♣ 76
                SOUTH
              ♠ Q65
              ♥ QT
              ♦ 9543
              ♣ 9854
```

The contract is 6♠s by W and N leads the Q♣s. W can see 2 possible losers, 1 in ♥s and 1 in ♠s so one must consider a strip and throw-in. W takes the ♣ trick and leads a high spade to the A followed by the K♠s and the Q does not drop so he now has a Q♠ loser and a possible ♥ loser. Now it is time to try a strip and throw-in. W now plays the top ♣s, ♦s and ♥s and notes the QT♥s drop which suggests S is out of ♥s. If S has the Q♠s then he can make the contract so W plays a low ♠ and S takes the trick but S has to play a ♣ or ♦ and W discards a losing heart and ruffs the trick in Dummy. Making 12 tricks.

    This is much easier to detect and play than a Squeeze. Clearly, the contract will fail if the ♥s split 3:3 which is less likely than 4:2 or if the three ♠s are with at least 3♥s. There is a principle here: if the contract will only make if the cards lie in specific positions then you must assume that they are in those positions and play for it. If they are not the contract fails but it also fails for all your competitors.

### 8.4.3 The Bath Coup as Declarer and Defender.

This an interesting and well know example of a particular hand; I shall show, unusually, how to play it and defend against it in the same section rather than split it between two chapters. I have taken the example from {16} with some modification.

|  | NORTH<br>♠ AQ95<br>♥ 652<br>♦ KJ3<br>♣ JT7 |  |
|---|---|---|
| WEST<br>♠ 973<br>♥ KQT94<br>♦ 92<br>♣ A53 | W N E S<br>　　　P 1♣<br>1♥ 1♠ P 1NT<br>P 3NT P P<br>P | EAST<br>♠ JT82<br>♥ 83<br>♦ AT864<br>♣ 92 |
|  | SOUTH<br>♠ K6<br>♥ AJ7<br>♦ Q75<br>♣ KQ864 |  |

From the Declarer's point of view, W leads the K♥s and S knows this must be from the top of a broken sequence, he does not have KQJ, based upon the cards he holds and the bidding. If S goes up with the A, he may loose 4♥s, a ♣ and a ♦, going 2 off. If S plays the 7, W has a dilemma and needs to find the ♦ lead to succeed. S has maximised his chances of success by ducking.

From the Defender's point of view, E should play the 8♥s and S plays the 7 as he is aware of the Bath Coup. What does W make of the 8 of ♥s? From the bidding S must have a ♥ stop which must surely be the A so the 8 cannot be encouraging in ♥s. If E had the A he would overtake the K and send back a ♥. It is unlikely to be requesting a ♠ so it is most likely to be suggesting a ♦. If W leads a ♦, S cannot make the contract as E returns a ♥ and whatever S plays W will regain the lead with the A♣ and follow up with 2 winning small ♥s. On the second trick a lead of a ♠ or ♣ is fatal for the Defenders.

Contents

# Chapter 9 Playing as Defenders

To defend effectively, you must have a system of signalling and discards. I shall repeat myself, this is not an encyclopaedia of Bridge but an explanation of how and why I play the game. You should also have a clear decision making process for choosing your lead.

A reminder from Chapter 7:

> *Remember the auction*
> *Note the lead*
> *Estimate the splits*
> *Keep track of the cards*
> *Finesse or Drop*

Finally you should use all techniques to build up a picture of your partner's and declarer's hands and keep track of the cards and hand shapes. See sections 8.1.1 and 8.1.3 above.

It is well to note that I shall considered both hands and the most likely place to make tricks. This is often in your partner's hand and you should lead on that basis. Defending is very much a team game with the highest number of uncertainties and so more difficult than being declarer but rewarding if you can make one more trick than anyone else in the room, it gives you a top in duplicate.

There are many hands where anyone who has learnt the basics of playing bridge will bid the right contract and make the same number of tricks: there is nothing you can do about it. Everyone gets an average score for such boards. It is these boards that ensure the range of results is limited to 30 to 70 % in Duplicate. I shall ignore such hands in the examples.

For those who feel reading how numerous hands should be bid and played, without any clear structure is useful, see {7}. Not my cup of tea.

## 9.1 Discards and Signalling

### 9.1.1 Conventions

Signals of suit length and preference are very important when defending. When leading a suit for the first time count signals are important although they come after sequences and broken sequences. However, when your partner leads and you cannot try to win the trick, your card should be a suit indicators. For example:

K♠ A♠ ? , your card should be a suit indicator

In general, once you have made one suit switch signal you don't need to make another.

#### 9.1.1.1 Count signals

Leading a new suit should always bear in mind a suit count so from a doubleton lead HL, three card suit, mud (middle up down), $4^{th}$ from an honour and second of four rags are all count signals. The third player cannot give count signals but can often indicate a suit preference.

#### 9.1.1.2 Suit signals in suit contracts

It is important to indicate one suit preference as soon as possible and maybe too late when you have to discard, this leads to the idea of :

**McKinney Indicators**

Partner leads high or Dummy takes it: your card should be a
*McKinney Indicator.*
Partner leads low to your bid suit, Dummy wins it, your card should be a
*McKinney Indicator.*
Partner leads an Ace, your card should be a
*McKinney Indicator.*

Definition of a *McKinney Indicator:*
a) Low card: suggests change to lower of two possible suits,
b) High card: suggests change to higher of two possible suits.

#### 9.1.1.3 Suit signals in NT contracts:

Obviously, it is more difficult in NT as there are three suits but your partner should be sensitive to the difficulty and it is often obvious that there is a suit that is out due to the contents of Dummy or the bidding leaving only two important suits.

Partner leads high or Dummy takes high
a) Medium to low card discourages this suit, encourages change of suit.
b) High card encourages continue with this suit. Often it is unblocking the suit.

In general Defenders are only interested in establishing one long suit. If partner gives a discourage signal on the first trick, player on opening lead should think about what other suit may be their best bet to make tricks taking note of the bidding, his hand and Dummy.

### 9.1.1.4 Discard signals are McKinney,

Clearly, a ruff is not a discard, a discard is when you cannot follow suit and throw away an unwanted card, these can be used to signal in both suit and NT contracts. The definition of McKinney discards is
a) I do not want the suit discarded.
  a1) High card indicates I want the higher of two outstanding suits.
  a2) Low card indicates I want the lower of two outstanding suits.
However if a suit switch signal has already been sent you can discard whatever you don't want.

### 9.1.2 Double as a signal.

Your partner may X a conventional bid to indicate a lead preference. e.g

```
1NT P 2♣ X 2♥ P 3NT P P P  or
1NT P 2♣ P 2♦ X 4♠ P P P
```

The 2♣ bid and the 2♦ bids are both conventional and do not indicate a suit so the X indicates: I would like you to lead the doubled suit when you can.

In the first bidding sequence the contract is 3NT by S and W is on lead and can lead a ♣. In the second sequence, the contact is 4♠ by N and E is on lead and can lead a ♦.

### 9.2 Rule of 11

As a Defender you can also use the **Rule of Eleven.** The Rule of Eleven says that when a low card is led from a new four, or more, card suit you should subtract the rank of the card from 11. The result is the number of cards higher than the card led that reside in the hands you can see plus those in the declarer's Here is an example with S as declarer:

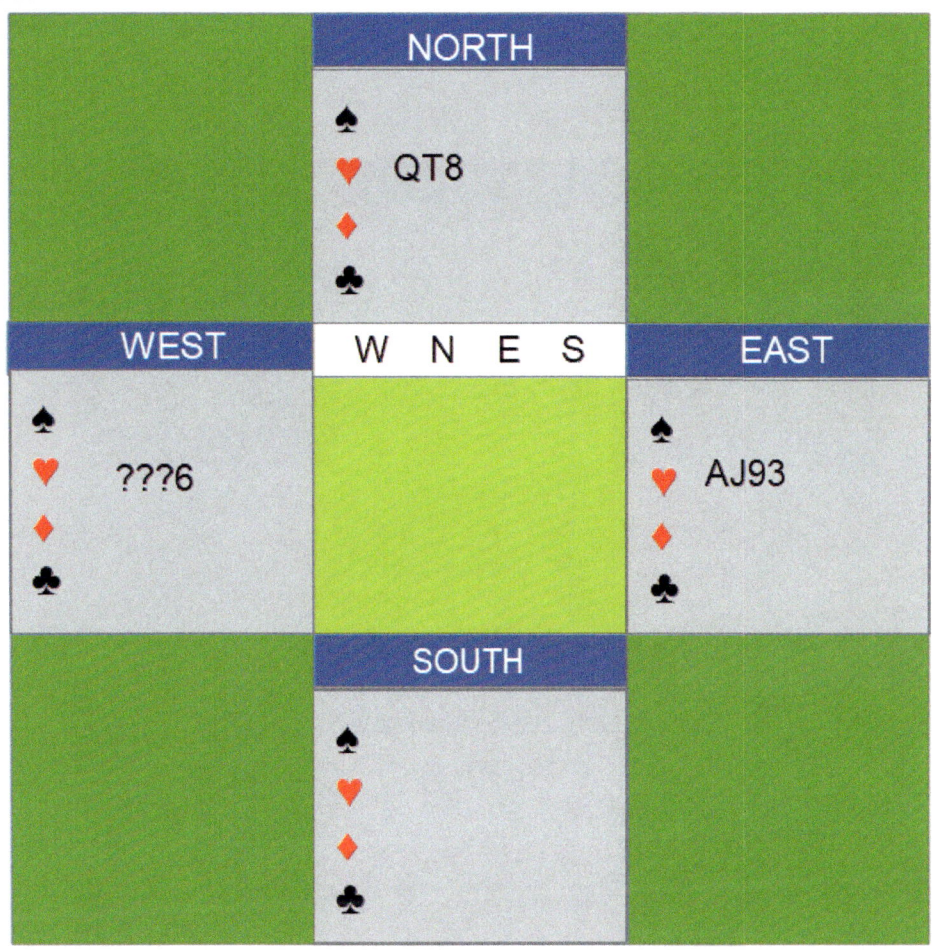

```
                    NORTH
                    ♠
                    ♥ QT8
                    ♦
                    ♣
     WEST        W  N  E  S        EAST
     ♠                              ♠
     ♥ ???6                         ♥ AJ93
     ♦                              ♦
     ♣                              ♣
                    SOUTH
                    ♠
                    ♥
                    ♦
                    ♣
```

Your partner uses standard leads and the 6 is likely to be from a four card suit. Using the Rule of 11, 11-6 says there are 5 cards higher that the 6 and as E you can see 6 cards higher than the 6 so S cannot have any cards higher than the 6. He must have two out of 2,3 & 4. E covers whichever

107

card N plays and S follows with a low card. W notes the cards played and has a complete picture of the suit.

### 9.3 Leading through Strength.

On either the first lead or later leads, it makes sense to lead through a perceived strength. What does this mean? The weakest case is when Dummy was bidding, he bid a suit denied by his partner who later became Declarer, e.g.

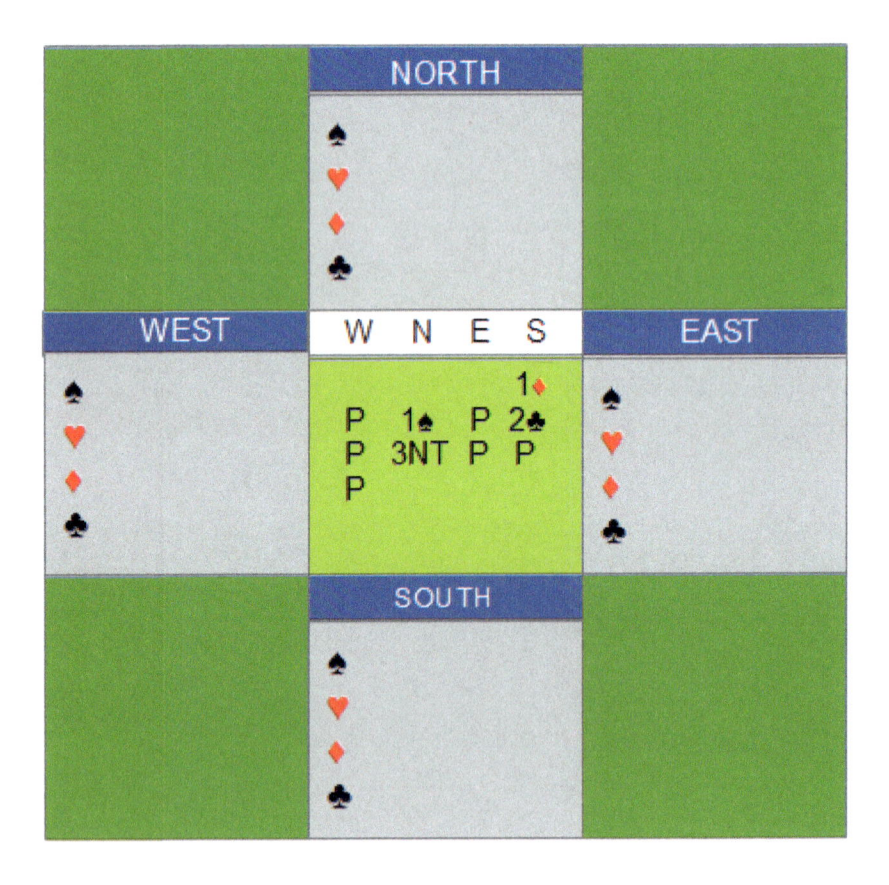

|  | W | N | E | S |
|---|---|---|---|---|
|  |  |  |  | 1♦ |
|  | P | 1♠ | P | 2♣ |
|  | P | 3NT | P | P |
|  | P |  |  |  |

The contract is 3NT by N and E leads a low ♥, the unbid suit, the trick is won by W who unfortunately has no more hearts so has to lead a ♣, ♦ or ♠. The Dummy, S has the AQ♣ and AQ♦ so a lead in ♣s or ♦s would finesse his partner, E, a very bad lead; whereas leading a ♠ may well finesse N. There are two important points here, 1), never finesse your partner and 2), try to finesse the opposition. If W has a chance to signal and asks for a ♦ then surly partner will have the K♦ but he does not want ♦s led.

Rather than lead the unbid suit, E can lead a ♣. This is **leading through strength**. S is known to have at least 4 ♣ s and 5 ♦ s and the bidding suggest N is depending upon S to cover ♣ s and ♦ s so must have ♥ controls to enable his 3NT bid. By leading ♥s you may be finessing your partner so the ♣ lead is more likely to finesse S and is therefore a better lead.

### 9.4 The play as a defender against NT.

The first action, as a defender, is to lead a card. This is often a crucial decision so should not be taken lightly. The subsequent play of the hand is also important and can be split into various strategies.

### 9.4.1 The choice of suit to lead.

On half the hands you play, you will have to chose a suit and card to lead, normally in that order but it can be a circular decision because there are some very bad leads. The commonest and most sensible lead is the un-bid suit where three suits have been bid or a major when no suits have been bid. When choosing which suit to lead, the cards in the suit may not provide a suitable lead. Here, again, refer to the standard leads listed on the EBU System card in Appendix E. They have become standard leads because experience has shown that they are the least likely to give away an unnecessary trick and most likely to gain you extra tricks. It is useful to compare the two tables: the NT section implies it is wrong to lead from an AK doubleton (but see an example below) and you might under lead an ace. I would put it more strongly, it is wrong to under lead an ace against a suit contract whilst it is almost recommended against an NT contract. In suit contracts voids and singletons are highly likely as they will be used to arrive at the final contract. In an NT contract they are unusual and you are looking to establish a long suit where the final low cards will be winners because they cannot be ruffed so you are happy to lose one or two tricks in the suit so long as you can get back in to make the length.

I regard leading the A from AKxx (and not bad from AK but lead the K) is an excellent lead as it allows you to look at Dummy without any cost to the defenders and allows you to assess your partners response. A common bidding sequence is 1NT P 3NT P P P and now you have to decide what to lead. The first step is to assume opener has 12 HCPs and responder also has 13 HCPs, add you own and deduct from 40; this tells you how many points your partner has. As the responder has not used Stayman nor a transfer he unlikely to have more than 3 cards in any major suit. Most weak 1NT openers exclude a 5 card major so your opponents do not have a major card fit and should be playing NTs. This also suggests the lead of a major is a good choice and which one depends upon your holding. With five or more low cards and a weak hand you are unlikely to get back in after the suit is established. On such a hand, it is better to lead a short major expecting your partner to have more than four cards and an honour for entry outside of the two majors. Having decided the suit the choice of card comes from the standard leads.

Lets consider some examples; in each case the bidding goes 1NT P 3NT P P P:

|       | NORTH |       |
|-------|-------|-------|
|       | ♠     |       |
|       | ♥     |       |
|       | ♦     |       |
|       | ♣     |       |

| WEST | W N E S | EAST |
|------|---------|------|
| ♠ T9876 |         1NT | ♠ |
| ♥ A32 | P 3NT P P | ♥ |
| ♦ Q32 | P | ♦ |
| ♣ J3 |   | ♣ |

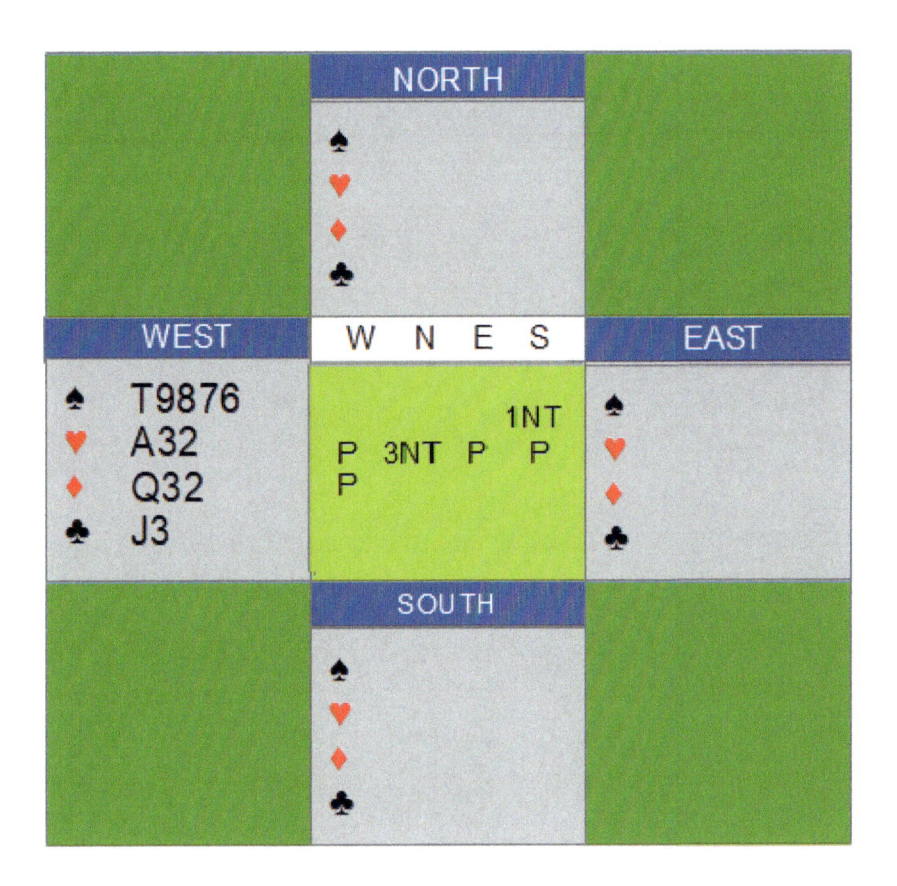

|       | SOUTH |       |
|-------|-------|-------|
|       | ♠     |       |
|       | ♥     |       |
|       | ♦     |       |
|       | ♣     |       |

The ♠s are likely to split 4:3:2 and N will not have 4 as he did not bid Stayman, so you hope your partner has 4 and I would lead the 7 as 4$^{th}$ highest but you could lead T as top of a sequence with these cards it makes little difference. The hope is that E has a honour in ♠ and two round of ♠s will take out their honours (controls) and W is set up for 3 ♠ tricks and 1 heart trick. Once the ♠s are cleared, E wins a trick and W has signalled for a ♥ , E plays a ♥  and W takes 4 tricks and the contract is 1 off.
Lets change the hand a little:

|        | NORTH |        |
|--------|-------|--------|
|        | ♠     |        |
|        | ♥     |        |
|        | ♦     |        |
|        | ♣     |        |

| WEST | W N E S | EAST |
|------|---------|------|
| ♠ T98765 |       1NT | ♠ |
| ♥ J32    | P 3NT P P | ♥ |
| ♦ Q3     | P         | ♦ |
| ♣ J3     |           | ♣ |

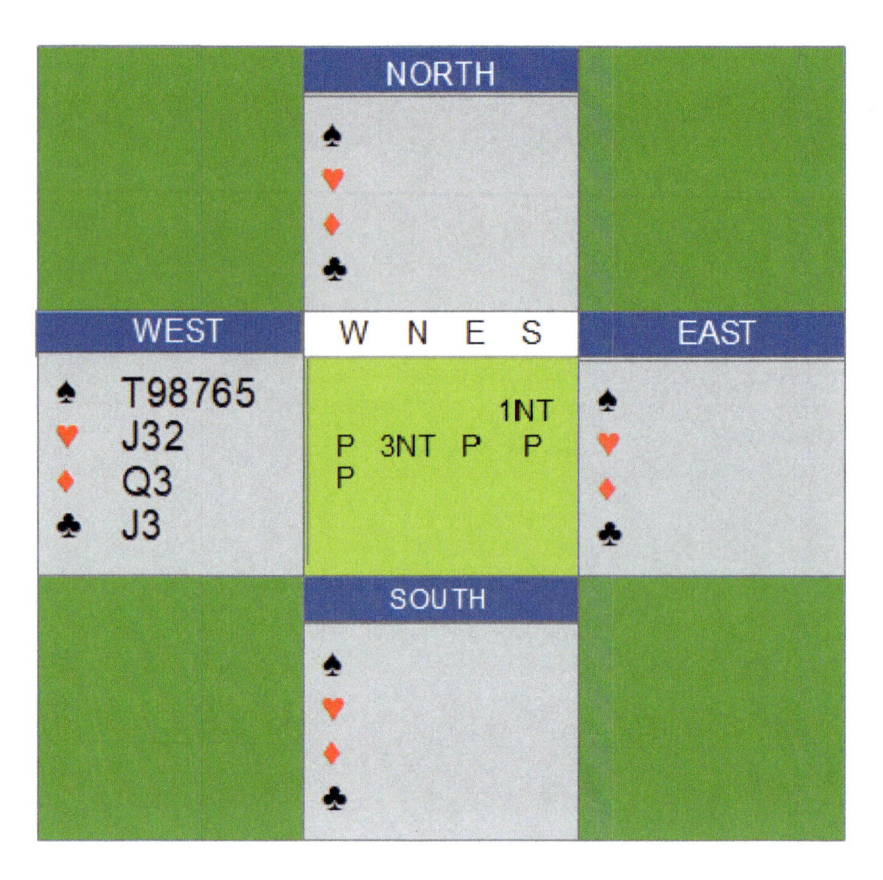

|        | SOUTH |        |
|--------|-------|--------|
|        | ♠     |        |
|        | ♥     |        |
|        | ♦     |        |
|        | ♣     |        |

Now W has a longer ♠ suit but has no entry so 3♥ is a better lead and W hopes that E has at least 5♥s and an entry with his 11 HCPs.
Another, hand with the same biding:

|       | NORTH |       |
|-------|-------|-------|
|       | ♠     |       |
|       | ♥     |       |
|       | ♦     |       |
|       | ♣     |       |

| WEST | W N E S | EAST |
|------|---------|------|
| ♠ J987 |       1NT | ♠ |
| ♥ 432 | P 3NT P P | ♥ |
| ♦ 53 | P | ♦ |
| ♣ AKJ3 |  | ♣ |

|       | SOUTH |       |
|-------|-------|-------|
|       | ♠     |       |
|       | ♥     |       |
|       | ♦     |       |
|       | ♣     |       |

Here I would always lead the A♣ to have a look at Dummy and then re-think my plan. Dummy appears with a long solid ♦ suit and above average HCPs, I would cash the K and then lead 7♠s. If you don't cash the K and let them in they may make 12 tricks. I remember playing against an International, many years ago, with a hand like this and opened with the 7♠s, thinking I shall make the AK later, however she took the first trick and the next 12 tricks. The traveller appeared and every one in the room hand taken two tricks so we got a bottom. A salutary lesson.

    When they have bid a suit and the suit bidder is on your left, a reasonable lead is the suit bid as his partner does not like the suit and if you are weak in the suit your partner should have strength sitting over the suit bidder. Leading through strength.

A different bidding sequence is :

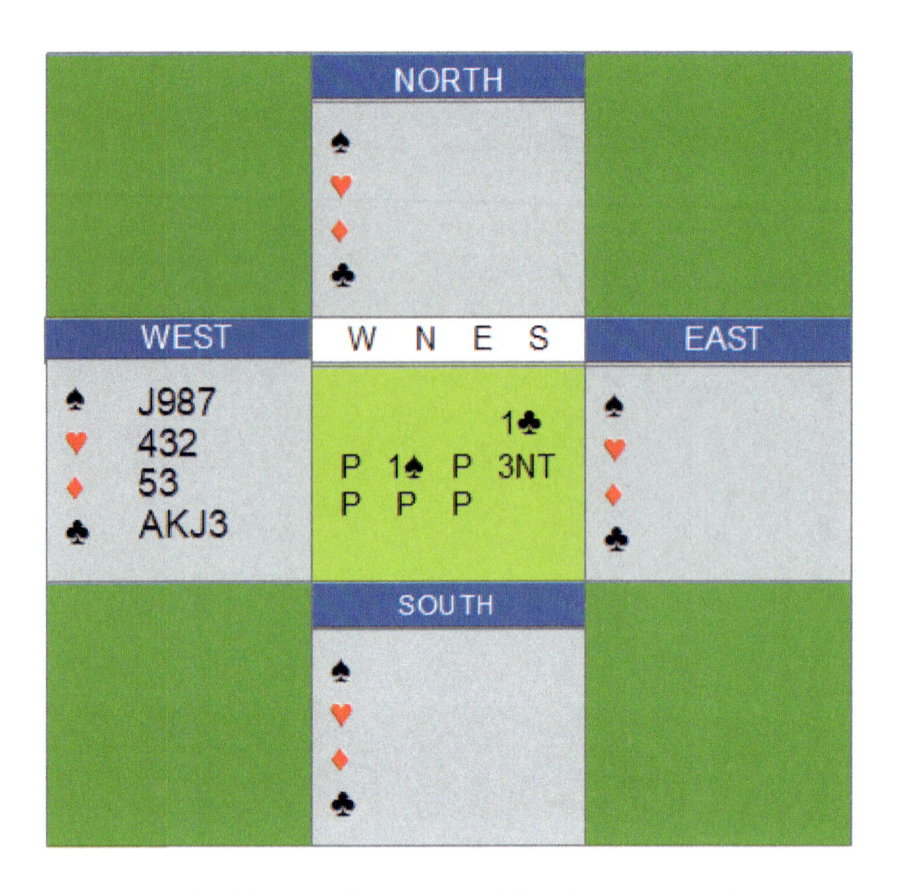

|  | WEST | | W | N | E | S | | EAST |
|---|---|---|---|---|---|---|---|---|
| ♠ | J987 | | | | | 1♣ | ♠ | |
| ♥ | 432 | | P | 1♠ | P | 3NT | ♥ | |
| ♦ | 53 | | P | P | P | | ♦ | |
| ♣ | AKJ3 | | | | | | ♣ | |

S is a strong hand with 19 HCPs and confident in ♣s, ♦s and ♥s so your only hope is that your partner is strong in ♠s so lead the 7♠s. A more complex bidding sequences is:

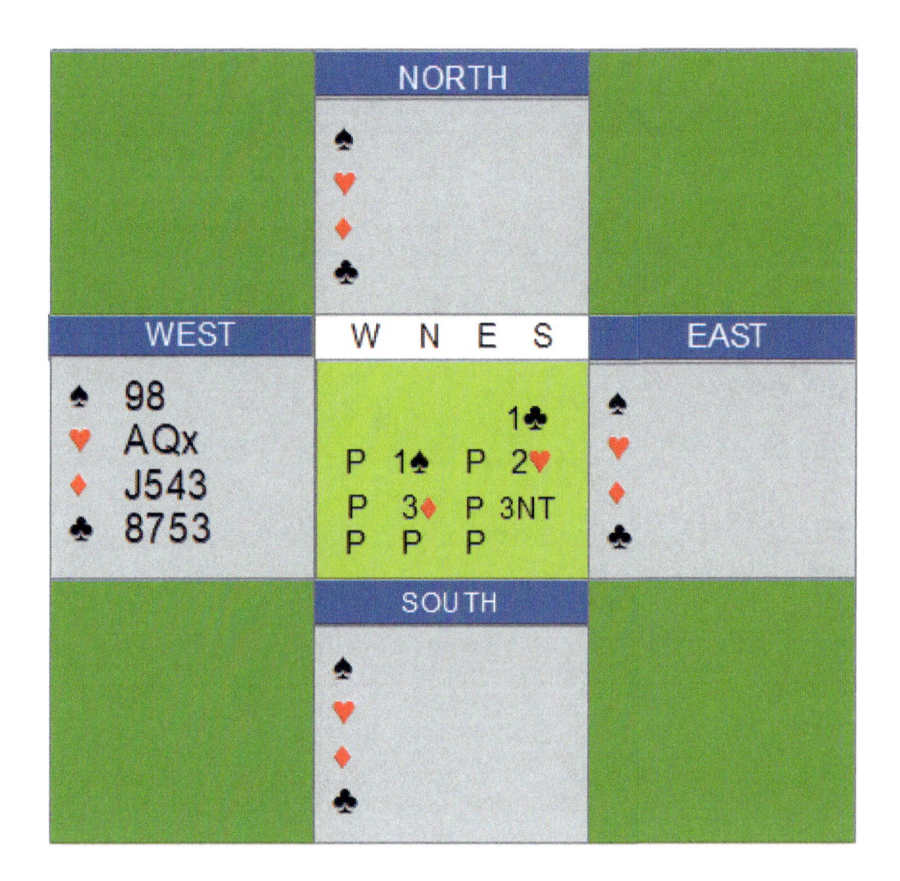

|  | NORTH |  |
|---|---|---|
| WEST ♠ 98 ♥ AQx ♦ J543 ♣ 8753 | W N E S<br>　　　　1♣<br>P 1♠ P 2♥<br>P 3♦ P 3NT<br>P P P | EAST |
|  | SOUTH |  |

The 3♦ bid is 4$^{th}$ suit forcing and asking S for a stopper in ♠s to enable a NT contract. W must not lead a ♥ as this will give away a trick. Leading a ♣ is likely to finesse his partner and the bidding shows S has a ♦ control. This leaves ♠s as the obvious choice but it is also sound because S will have few ♠s and E may have strength over N. You are hoping to finesse N.

### 9.4.2 Establishing the Defenders Longest suit.

In NT contracts the major approach is to establish the partnership longest suit. Although this is true, it is possible that partner has a second suit with guaranteed winners so if he wins the first trick and changes suit it is an indicator he has such a suit and partner should take note, e.g.

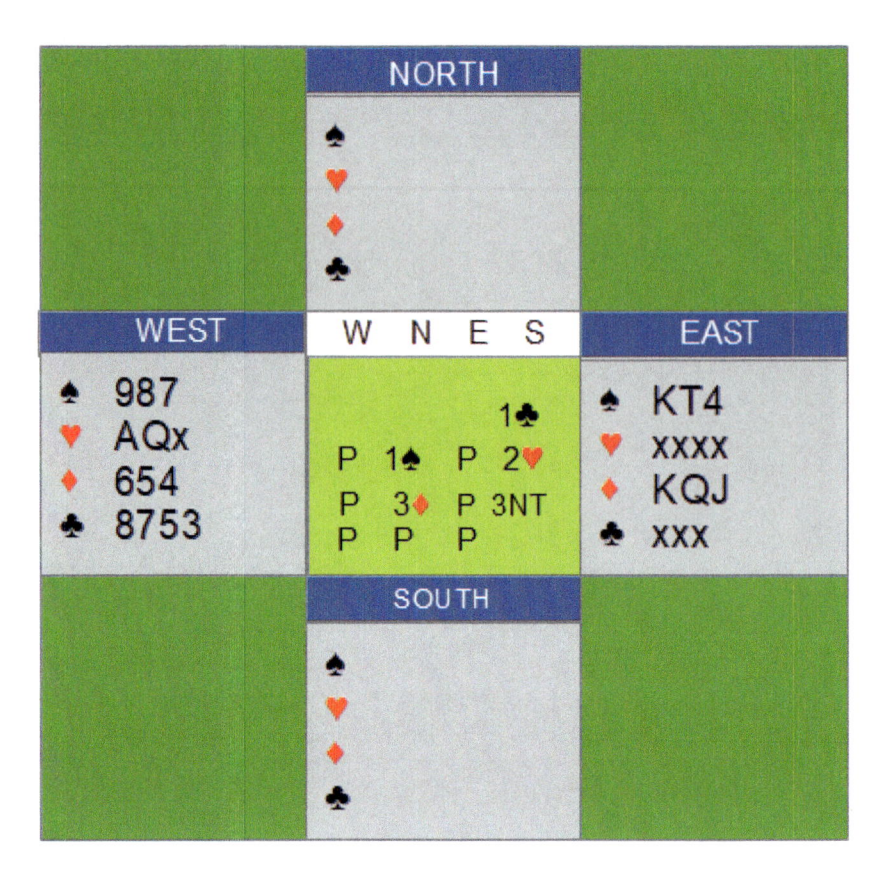

```
           NORTH
           ♠
           ♥
           ♦
           ♣

WEST      W  N  E  S       EAST
♠ 987              1♣      ♠ KT4
♥ AQx     P  1♠  P  2♥     ♥ xxxx
♦ 654     P  3♦  P  3NT    ♦ KQJ
♣ 8753    P  P   P         ♣ xxx

           SOUTH
           ♠
           ♥
           ♦
           ♣
```

W leads the 8♠ and Dummy has the AQxx♠s and S must have 2 ♠s. S plays the Q♠ to maintain control and E takes the trick with the K♠ but leads the K♦s. Note W has finessed Dummy. Now W can signal for ♥ with 6♦s so now W knows E has ♠s and at least two tricks in ♦ s and E knows W has a good ♥ combination, all this after two tricks. I am not commenting on the best play for the Declarer as this section is about defending.

### 9.4.3 Managing your long suit, avoid Blocking

A common auction, 1NT P 3NT P P P only makes 67% of the time so when the contract goes off it is not time reconsider your bidding system or descend into naval gazing, just shrug and move on. This is most likely to happen when both hands are 4432 and the doubleton is in the same suit but it can also happen on other hands:

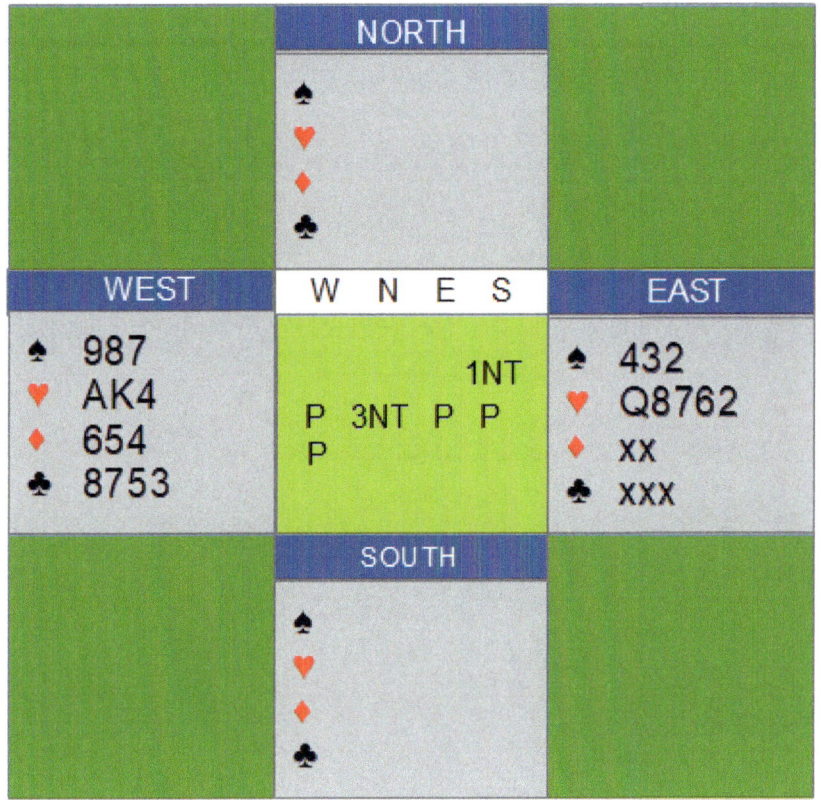

|  | NORTH | |
|---|---|---|
| | ♠ ♥ ♦ ♣ | |
| **WEST** | W N E S | **EAST** |
| ♠ 987<br>♥ AK4<br>♦ 654<br>♣ 8753 |        1NT<br>P 3NT P P<br>P | ♠ 432<br>♥ Q8762<br>♦ xx<br>♣ xxx |
| | SOUTH | |
| | ♠ ♥ ♦ ♣ | |

W leads the A♥ and receives an encourage signal from E as he plays the 8♥. W plays K♥ and E knows W has a third ♥ as he played AK and that NS must be 3:2 as they have both bid NT. W plays the 4♥, E plays the Q and the J must drop from N or S so EW make the first 5 tricks. Note, the important concept of **Unblocking** is shown here. Many people say you should play your A first and then a low card showing you started with AK and your partner plays accordingly but in this case E would have to play the Q on the second round and return a ♥ won by W. Now W cannot lead back to E in ♥s and the suit is blocked.

### 9.4.4 Avoiding their suits

Consider a more complicated auction where you also have a long suit, in NT you are always trying to establish the partnerships long suit:

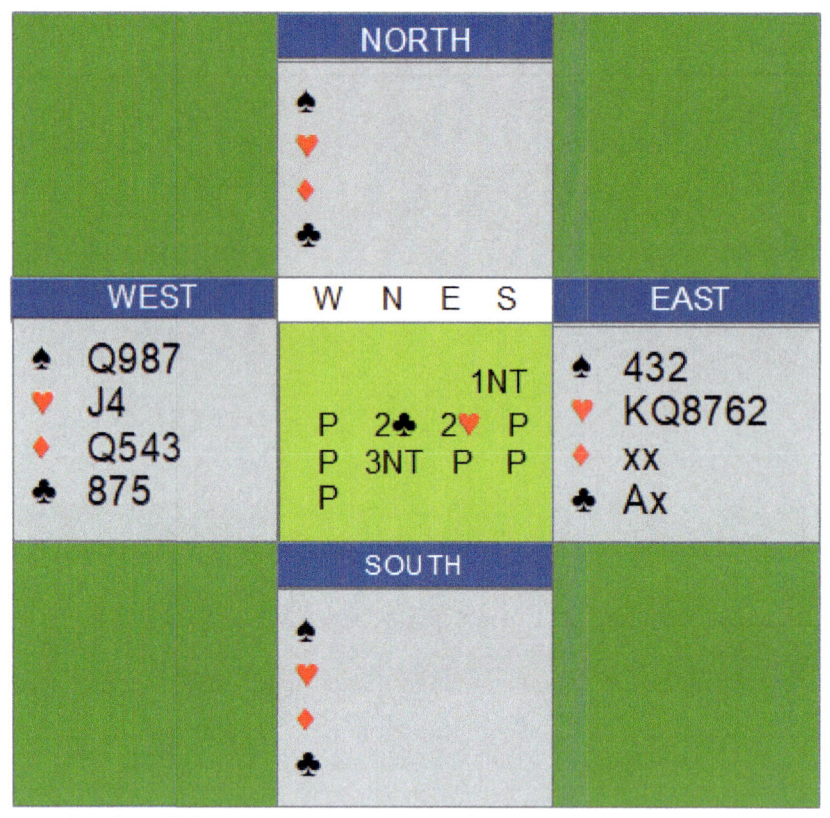

|  | NORTH<br>♠<br>♥<br>♦<br>♣ |  |
|---|---|---|
| **WEST**<br>♠ Q987<br>♥ J4<br>♦ Q543<br>♣ 875 | W N E S<br>          1NT<br>P 2♣ 2♥ P<br>P 3NT P P<br>P | **EAST**<br>♠ 432<br>♥ KQ8762<br>♦ xx<br>♣ Ax |
|  | SOUTH<br>♠<br>♥<br>♦<br>♣ |  |

W is on lead and knows E has 6 good ♥s and 10-15 HCPs but most likely 10-12 because of his own points. You can not lead a low ♠ as N must have 4 ♠s as he bid Staymen with 13 HCPs. W leads his partners suit, always the first preference, with the J♥s both to unblock the ♥s and tell his partner where the J is. Now the race is on, E plays a low♥ and S takes it with the A from N or S. If S can make 9 tricks without relying on ♣s he sails home and makes the contract. However, if he needs club tricks, E takes the A♣s and 4 ♥ tricks and beats the contract.

## 9.5 Playing as a defender against a suit contract

### 9.5.1 Leads and Signals

All the usual rules apply: remember the auction and decide where the opposition points are and where some of the suits are.

Consider your own hand and estimate your partner's strength. Now you can chose a suit to lead. If your partner has bid a suit the choice is simple, lead his suit otherwise you must make an educated guess. I have read, "do not lead a high card in partner's suit because it may cost a trick;" I do not agree with this where your partner made an overcall. He is likely to have one or two honours in the suit and would like to know where the rest are. You lead an honour and on seeing the cards in Dummy, he will know where all the honours are and play appropriately. When your partner was the opening bidder but you are defending it would wrong to lead an honour in your partner's suit as it may be a very poor suit. Context is always important.

Losing the first trick should be seen as an opportunity to give your partner a suit signal. You have already suggested one suit, the first suit led and it is unlikely that you or your partner want the suit the opponent has led so this leaves just two suits. Either of you, particularly the one who can't win the trick, should play a card that indicates your other suit via a McKinney indicator. For example you lead a ♥ and the trick was won by the declarer, he leads a ♦ to the ace on the table so you can play a high ♦ showing ♠s, or a low ♦ showing ♣s and your partner can do the same. This means, by the second trick you each have a sufficient description of each others hand and you can ignore signals for the rest of the hand.

With AK and nothing else in one suit, play the K, see standard leads, followed by the A. You will win both tricks except in very rare circumstances about which we will not worry. Playing them in the wrong order tells your partner it is a AK doubleton and he will have played a McKinney indicator on the K. Many authors say do it on the A but if you are making a general use of McKinney indicators it is consistent for your partner to play it on the K because he can't win the trick. Within two tricks you have information on your partner's hand. It is rare to have two good suits in one hand so one signal is enough.

When there is no clear information on what suit to lead you can fall back on what cards you hold in each suit. In an auction such as

> 1♠ P 4♠ P P
> P

you have very little to go on although with three difficult suits you may decide to lead trumps unless you have a trump holding that you want declarer to play through. In general leading a trump does not cost you a trick but hands the initiative to the declarer. Under leading an ace, from Axxx, is almost a capital crime followed by the petty felony of leading an unsupported ace, Axxx, and the minor crime of under leading a K. Good leads are leading the top of a sequence or the top of a broken sequence. Quite often it is a case of leading the least worse suit using the card set by standard leads.

With the play underway and few alternatives you may lead through strength on the table if you are Declarer's LHO or to the table's weak suit if you are Declarer's RHO. These often gain nothing and cost nothing but hand the initiative back to the Declarer.

As the hand is played your initial estimation of each hand is clarified by the cards played and you can decide whether a suit is likely to be ruffed, You may chose to force a ruff to decease Declarer's holding and establish your own honours.

### 9.5.2 Forcing Defence

You hold, say AKQx in ♠s and lead the A♠s, your partner signals he has a ♥ suit, S plays the J and there are 4 ♠s and 3 poor ♦s in Dummy.

|  | NORTH<br>♠<br>♥<br>♦<br>♣ |  |
|---|---|---|
| WEST<br>♠ AKQ7<br>♥ K43<br>♦ 54<br>♣ 7532 | W　N　E　S<br>　　　　　1♦<br>P　1♠　P　2♣<br>P　3♦　P　P<br>P | EAST<br>♠ 5432<br>♥ Q876<br>♦ Kxx<br>♣ xx |
|  | SOUTH<br>♠<br>♥<br>♦<br>♣ |  |

You decide to play a forcing defence so you play the K♠ and it is ruffed by Declarer with no surprise to you. It is likely from the bidding that Declarer now has 4 trumps and would like to ruff in the short side before drawing trumps. You win the next trick and play the Q♠ forcing another ♦ out of Declarer. This may have created ♦ winners in your or your partners a hand.

The forcing defence should not be confused with a ruff and discard. A rough and discard occurs when declarer is out of cards of one suit in both his hands. You play that suit and Declarer decides he wants the lead in Dummy so he ruffs it in Dummy and discards a loser from his own hand, you have generally given Declarer an extra trick.

### 9.5.3 Long Suits in a suit contract

Lets take an example from above but with a different auction and contract to compare defensive play in a suit versus NT.

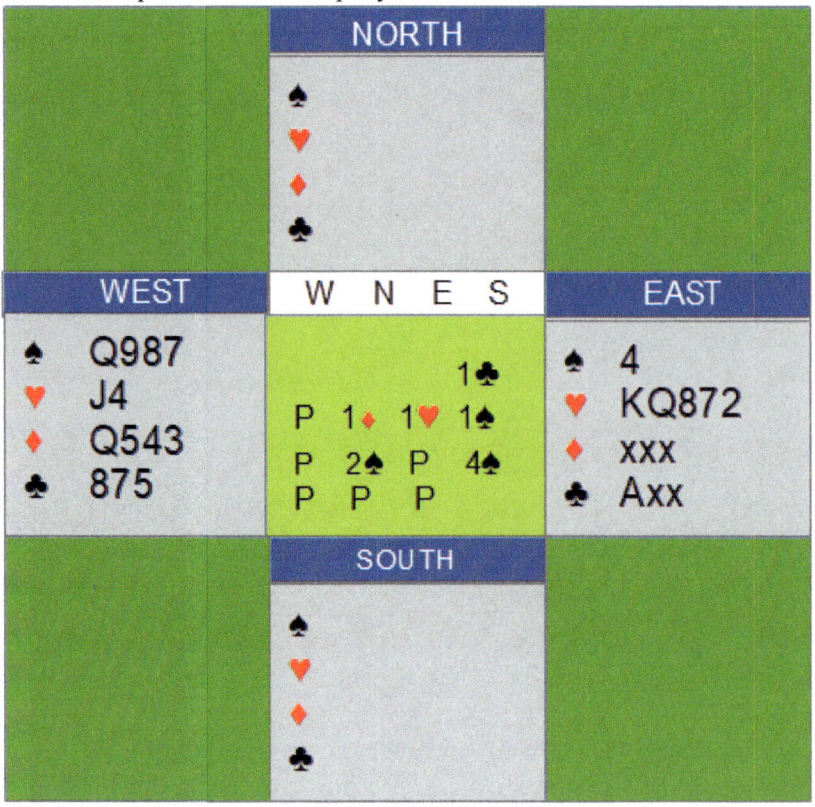

|  | NORTH |  |
|---|---|---|
| ♠ | | |
| ♥ | | |
| ♦ | | |
| ♣ | | |

| WEST | W N E S | EAST |
|---|---|---|
| ♠ Q987 |           1♣ | ♠ 4 |
| ♥ J4 | P 1♦ 1♥ 1♠ | ♥ KQ872 |
| ♦ Q543 | P 2♠ P 4♠ | ♦ xxx |
| ♣ 875 | P P P | ♣ Axx |

|  | SOUTH |  |
|---|---|---|
| ♠ | | |
| ♥ | | |
| ♦ | | |
| ♣ | | |

Now W is on lead and the bidding suggests NS have 8♠s so W leads his partner's suit and plays the J♥ to show him where the honour is. Usually NS will take the trick with the A♥ and hope to ditch a ♥ from the hand with only 2 ♥s. E plays the 2♥s as a suit signal. It can't be discouraging because it his best suit so it is a McKinney indicator showing an interest in ♣s. EW are hoping to make at least 1♥, 1♠ and 1♣ trick and maybe a ♦ trick. The outcome will depend upon the distribution of cards between N and S but the initial approach is always the same : lead your partner's suit, partner signals if possible and E and W reassess their plans after seeing Dummy and the cards played on the first trick.

### 9.5.4 Detecting a Cross Ruff

You start out with the intention of using a forcing defence but find a singleton or void in Dummy in a different suit. This suggest Declarer may attempt to play a cross-ruff so you switch to a trump lead to reduce the trumps in both N and S. If you get in again before trumps have been drawn, you repeat the trump lead. Here is an example where the contract is 4♦s by S:

|  | NORTH |  |
|---|---|---|
|  | ♠ JT86 |  |
|  | ♥ 2 |  |
|  | ♦ 987 |  |
|  | ♣ KQJT2 |  |

| WEST | W N E S | EAST |
|---|---|---|
| ♠ AKQ7 |           1♦ | ♠ 5432 |
| ♥ K543 | P 1♠ P 2♦ | ♥ A876 |
| ♦ 53 | P 3♦ P 4♦ | ♦ K62 |
| ♣ 874 | P P P | ♣ 65 |

|  | SOUTH |  |
|---|---|---|
|  | ♠ 9 |  |
|  | ♥ QJT9 |  |
|  | ♦ AQJT4 |  |
|  | ♣ A93 |  |

W leads the A♠, Dummy plays the 6, E plays the 5 and finally S plays the 9. W considers the 9♠s from S and decides it is a singleton as it is the highest card he cannot see and the 5 from E is his top card so it is a ♥ signal. W plays the K♥, it holds, so EW have their ♥ trick before S can discard the 2♥ but W has set up a cross ruff for S so he plays the

4♦ to reduce the trumps in both hands. S makes 9 tricks for 1 off. If W continues with a forcing defence, S sets up the ♥s and makes 3 ♥ ruffs instead of 2. He then makes 10 tricks.

### 9.5.5 Long suit in Dummy and 1 entry

The contact is 4♥ and W is on lead at the 7$^{th}$ trick. You play to remove the entry in Dummy before the declarer can set up his long suit.

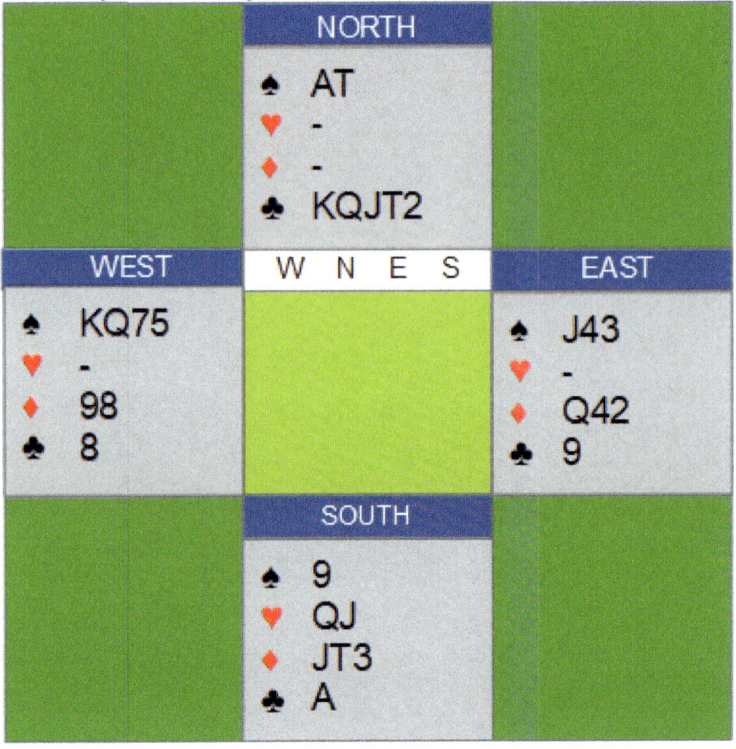

|  | NORTH<br>♠ AT<br>♥ -<br>♦ -<br>♣ KQJT2 |  |
|---|---|---|
| WEST<br>♠ KQ75<br>♥ -<br>♦ 98<br>♣ 8 | W  N  E  S | EAST<br>♠ J43<br>♥ -<br>♦ Q42<br>♣ 9 |
|  | SOUTH<br>♠ 9<br>♥ QJ<br>♦ JT3<br>♣ A |  |

W is on lead and must lead the K♠ to remove the A♠ in Dummy. S can only play a ♣ to the A♣ and is locked out of Dummy. You could consider this as creating a block.

### 9.5.6 Finessing Declarer

There are clear combinations of cards where you must not lead a suit as a defender depending up on the cards you can see. W on lead should not lead through a weak suit on the table. Whereas E can lead towards a weak suit in Dummy as either S or W will be strong. In the example below W would finesse his partner, a no-no, whilst E would finesse Declarer. E should lead this suit and W should not.

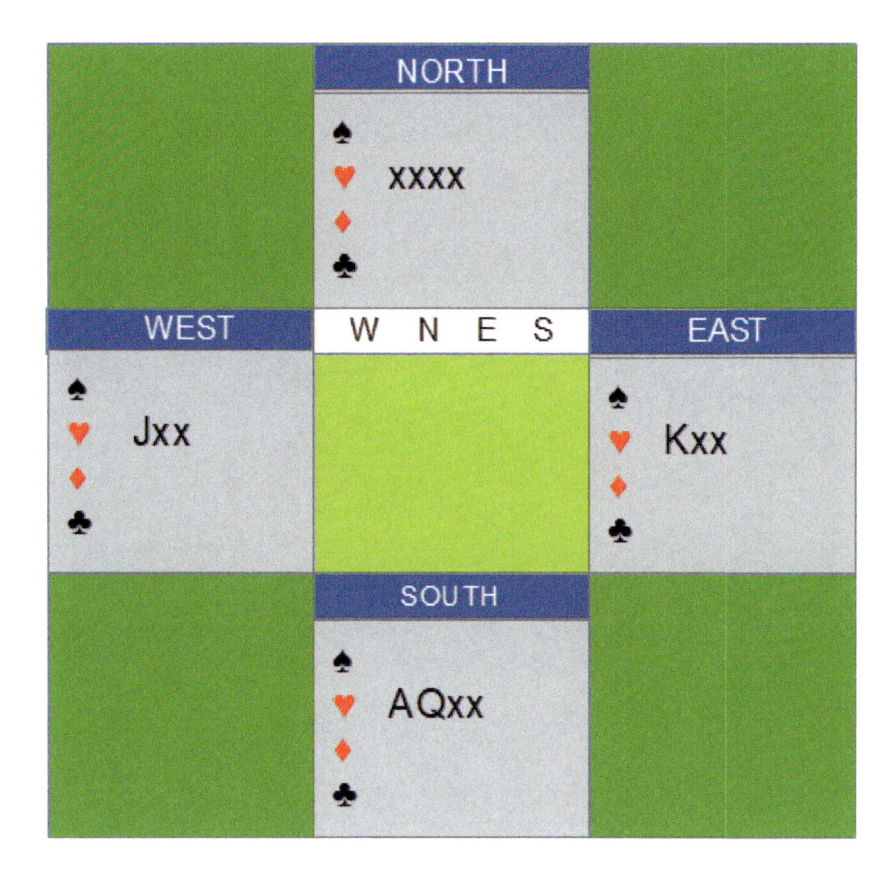

```
                    NORTH
                    ♠
                    ♥ xxxx
                    ♦
                    ♣
        WEST       W  N  E  S      EAST
        ♠                          ♠
        ♥ Jxx                      ♥ Kxx
        ♦                          ♦
        ♣                          ♣
                    SOUTH
                    ♠
                    ♥ AQxx
                    ♦
                    ♣
```

### 9.5.7 Ruff and Discard.

When you know declarer is void in both hands do not lead the void suit as Declarer can discard a loser from either hand and make an extra trick. The contract is in ♠ and the play has reached the position below and W is on lead:

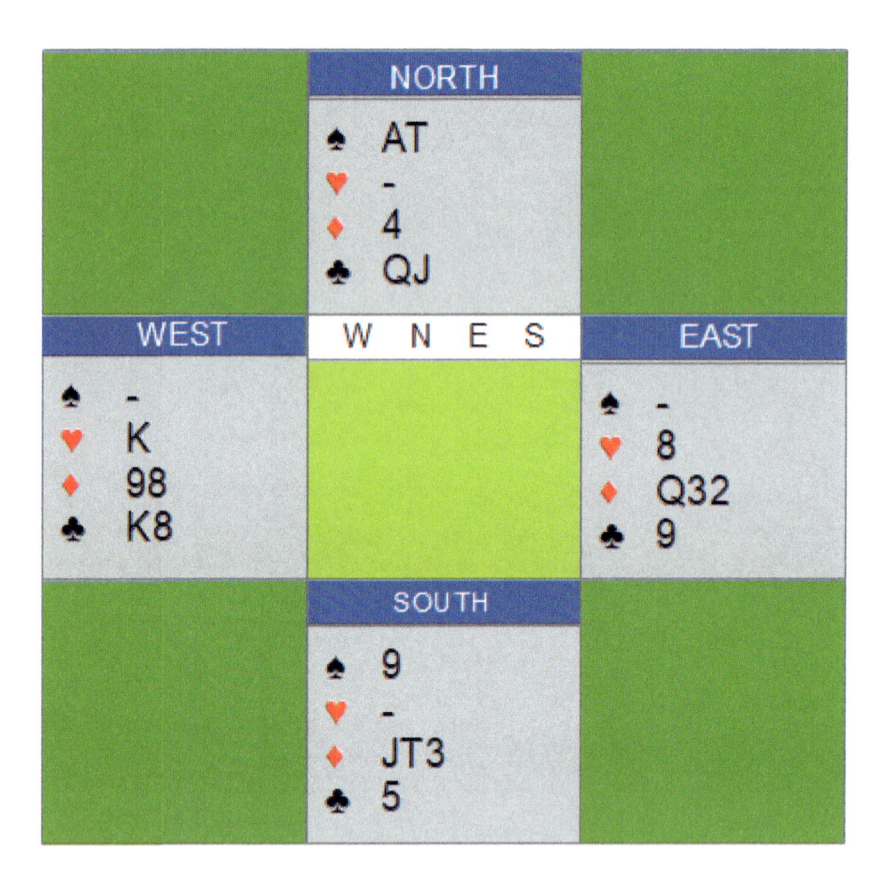

|  | NORTH<br>♠ AT<br>♥ -<br>♦ 4<br>♣ QJ |  |
|---|---|---|
| WEST<br>♠ -<br>♥ K<br>♦ 98<br>♣ K8 | W  N  E  S | EAST<br>♠ -<br>♥ 8<br>♦ Q32<br>♣ 9 |
|  | SOUTH<br>♠ 9<br>♥ -<br>♦ JT3<br>♣ 5 |  |

W knows the K♥s is boss and there is another ♥ in S or E, this makes a ♥ lead poor but if E has the ♥ it becomes an awful lead. The K♥s is led and S decides to discard 3♦s from Dummy and EW gain no tricks in ♦s. If W leads the 9♦s or the K♣s, EW take a ♣ and a ♦ trick. This could make the difference between a top and an average in Duplicate.

## 9.6 Things not to do as a Defender

*Never finesse your partner.*
*Never knowingly give your opponents a ruff and discard.*

Contents

## Appendix A

Frontispiece from Klinger {1} with minor modifications; note this is a starting point and details will be changed in this (my) book.

### THE BASICS
**Hand Valuation :**
High card points ( HCP) : A = 4 K = 3 Q = 2 J = 1

Length points: 1 for each card after the 4$^{th}$

Distributional points after a trump fit has been found :
Void = 3 Singleton = 2 Doubleton = 1

**Hand Shapes:**
Balanced patterns : 4-3-3-3  4-4-3-2  5-3-3-2
Semi-balanced patterns : 5-4-2-2  6-3-2-2  7-2-2-2
Unbalanced patterns : All other patterns.

**Points needed for games :**
3NT 4♥/♠ : 25 points  For 5♣/♦ : 29 points
**Points for slams** : Small slam ( any 6-contract) : 33 points
Grand slam ( any 7-contract) : 37 points

**Trumps needed for games and slams :**
At least an 8-card trump fit is required.

**Opening the bidding:** 0-11 points : Pass
12-21 points : Open with 1-bid  21-up: Open with 2-bid

**Which suit to open :**
1. Start with your longest suit.
2. With a 5-5 or 6-6 pattern, bid the higher-ranking suit first.
3. (a) 4-3-3-3 : Open 1NT or 2NT with the correct point count. If not. open the 4-card suit (or 2♣ if 23-up).
b) 4-4-3-2 pattern : Open 1NT or 2NT with the correct point count. Open 2♣ with 23 HCP or more. In the 15-19 zone, open the lower of 4-card suit.
c) 4-4-4-1 pattern : With a black singleton, open the middle suit. With a red singleton, open the suit below the singleton.

**1NT opening :** 12-14 points, balanced shape

**2NT opening :** 20-22 points, balanced shape

**With 23-up balanced :** Open 2♣ and rebid no-trumps next (unless you can support responder).

**Responding to a suit opening :** Single raise = 6-9 1NT response = 6-9 1-level suit reply = 6+ points. 2-level new suit reply = 10+ points. Jump-shift = 16+ points and a powerful one-suiter or a strong suit plus support for opener's suit. Jump-raise = 10-12 points, 4-card support 2NT response = 11-12, balanced 3NT response = 13-15 points, 4-3-3-3 pattern. Responder's change of suit is forcing (unless responder is a passed hand or there has been a 1NT bid in the auction).

**Responding to 1NT :** With a balanced hand. pass with 0-10. Bid 2NT with 11-12. Bid 3NT with 13-18 and explore slam with 19 or more. With an unbalanced hand. bid a suit at the 2-level with 0-10 points. jump to the 3-level or to game with a long suit and 11 HCP or more. Any suit bid over 1 NT shows a 5-card suit at least.

**Responding to 2NT:** With a balanced hand. pass with 0-3 points, bid 3NT with 4-10 points and explore slam with 11 points or more. The 2NT opening is not forcing but any reply commits the partnership to game. A suit bid at the 3-level shows a 5-card suit and is forcing.

**4NT Blackwood Convention asking for aces :**

5♣ = 0 or 4 aces 5♦ = 1 ace 5♥ = 2 aces 5♠ = 3 aces.

After the reply to 4NT. With all the aces a bid of 5NT asks for kings :

6♣ = 0 / 4 kings 6♦ = 1 king 6♥ = 2 kings 6♠ = 3 kings

**Overcalls :** A suit overcall at the 1-level shows a strong five-card or longer suit and 8-15 HCP. A suit overcall at the 2-level (not a jump overcall) shows a strong five-card or longer suit and 10-15 HCP. The 1NT overcall shows 15-18 points, balanced shape and at least 1 stopper in their suit. Doubling a suit at the 1-level or 2-level is for take out if partner has not bid. A double of no-trumps is for penalties.

**Leads:** Top from a sequence of 3 or more cards as long as the sequence contains at least 1 honour. 4th-highest from a long suit with no sequence. Top from a doubleton. Middle-up-down from 3 rags.

**Signals :** High-low is encouraging on partner's lead or as a discard. Lowest card is discouraging.

Contents

## Appendix B
### References and Bibliography

1 "Guide to Better Acol Bridge" by Ron Klinger and Andrew Kambites, Cassel & Co, London 2001.

2 "The New Complete Book of Bridge" by Albert Dormer with Ron Klinger, Victor Gollancz, London 1999.

3 "Acol in the 90s" by Terence Reese and David Bird Robert Hale, London 1990.

4 "Basic Bridge" by Ron Klinger, Pat Husband & Andrew Kambites Cassel & Co, London 2001

5 "Guide To Better Card Play" by Ron Klinger, Cassel & Co, London 2001.

6 "Hocus-Pocus" by Erwin Brecher, Panacea Press London 2001.

7 "Defence on the Other Hand" by David Bird and Larry Cohen, Master Point Press Toronto 2020.

8 "The Expert Improver" by Danny Roth, Collins Willow London1992

9 "Bridge Odds for Practical Players" by Hugh Kelsey and Michael Glauert, Cassel and Co London 2001.

10 "The Mathematical Theory of Bridge" by Émile Borel and André Chéron in English by Alec Traub and Giles Laurén Master Point Press Toronto 2017.

11 "Dormer on Deduction" by Albert Dormer, Cassel & Co. London 2001

12 "Understanding the Contested Auction" by Ron Klinger and Andrew Kambites, Cassel & Co. London 2001

13 "Squeeze Play Made Easy" by Terence Reese and Patrick Jourdain, Robert Hale Ltd London 1992.

14 "Bridge Conventions, Defences and Counter Measures" by Ron Klinger, Victor Gollancz London 1999.

15 "Cue-bidding to Slams" by Ron Klinger, Victor Gollancz London 1996.

16 "Bridge Winning Ways to Play Your Cards" by Paul Mendelson, Constable & Robinson London 2008.

17 "Playing With Trumps" by Sally Brock McGraw-Hill 1998.

18 https://www............ Search for any topic.      Contents

## Appendix C

## Tables

### Table 1  4441

4441 without interference
O1 is opener's 1st bid and O2 is openers 2nd bid, R1 is responder's 1st bid.

| Hand | O1 | R1 | O2 |
|---|---|---|---|
| 4♣ 4♦ 4♥ 1♠ | 1♣ | 1♦ | 1♥ |
|  |  | 1♥ | 2+♥ |
|  |  | 1♠ | 2♣ * |
| 4♣ 4♦ 1♥ 4♠ | 1♣ | 1♦ | 1♠ |
|  |  | 1♥ | 1♠ |
|  |  | 1♠ | 2+♠ |
| 4♣ 1♦ 4♥ 4♠ | 1♣ | 1♦ | 1♥ |
|  |  | 1♥ | 2+♥ |
|  |  | 1♠ | 2+♠ |
| 1♣ 4♦ 4♥ 4♠ | 1♦ | 1♥ | 2+♥ |
|  |  | 1♠ | 2+♠ |
|  |  | 2♣ | 2♦ * |

\* lie about a minor. With 15-16 HCP in the 4441 hand it is better to bid 1/2NT than repeat the minor as all suits are covered by the combined hand.

R1 bidding 1NT indicates no major and 8-10 HCP after 1♣ and no major and 6-9 HCP after 1♦.

4441 with interference

Responder bids normally if possible or 1NT with a stop in the interfering suit or X (Negative).

O2 after a X can bid a new suit and only imply 12+ points and a four card suit, without it being a reverse, therefore a jump change of suit or NT is used to show 16+ and 5:4.

e.g.   1♣ 1♠ X P 2♦ / ♥   Opener is only showing 12-15 HCP and 4♦ / ♥ s but may only have 4♣ s.

   1♣ 1♠ X P 3♦ ……. Opener is 5:4 and 16+

[Contents](#)

# Table 2 Responses to 1NT

### Table 2 Outline of the responses to 1NT opening bid

| Respond. 1 | Opener 2 | |
|---|---|---|
| 2♣/♦/♥ | | Stayman / Transfers see below |
| 2♠ | 2NT /3NT | Shows Responder has balanced 11 HCP precisely |
| 2NT | Pass/3NT | Shows Responder has balanced 12 HCP precisely |
| 3♦ ♣♥ ♠ | | 6+ card suit 18+ points, Slam try, at least Game in suit |
| 4♣ | | Gerber |

## Table 3 Transfers
### Table 3 Transfers after 1NT Opening bid
R1 is Responder's first bid, O2 is Opener's second bid etc.

| R1 | O2 | R2 | Strength and shape | |
|---|---|---|---|---|
| 2♦ | 2♥ | pass | 0-10 HCP, 5♥ | Invite Game in a major or NT |
| 2♦ | 2♥ | 2♠ | 11-12 HCP, 5♥ + 4♠ | Invite Game in ♥ or NT |
| 2♦ | 2♥ | 2NT | 11-12 HCP, 5♥ + less than 4♠ | Unbalanced, Game force in a suit |
| 2♦ | 2♥ | 3♣/♦ | 15+ HCP, 5♥ + 4♣/♦ | Invite Game in ♥ |
| 2♦ | 2♥ | 3♥ | 11-12 points, 6♥ or 5 good ♥ | Pass |
| 2♦ | 2♥ | 4♥ | 13-17 points 6♥ | 4♥ + 14 HCP; bids Game |
| 2♦ | 3♥ | Super-Acceptance by Opener shows | | 4♥ and 14 HCPs |
| 2♥ | 2♠ | pass | 0-10 HCP, 5♠ | Invite Game in ♠ or NT |
| 2♥ | 2♠ | 2NT | 11-12 HCP, 5♠ + less than 4♥ | Unbalanced, Game force in a suit |
| 2♥ | 2♠ | 3♣/♦ | 15+ HCP, 5♠ + 4♣/♦ | Invite Game in a major or NT |
| 2♥ | 2♠ | 3♥ | 11-12 HCP, 5♠ + 4♥ | Invite Game in ♠ |
| 2♥ | 2♠ | 3♠ | 11-12 points, 6♠ or 5 good ♠ | Pass |
| 2♥ | 2♠ | 4♠ | 13-16 points 6♠ | 4♠ + 14 HCP; bids Game |
| 2♥ | 3♠ | Super-acceptance by Opener shows | | 4♠ and 14 HCPs |

# Table 4  Stayman after 1NT opening and 2♣ response

O2 refers to Opener's second bid, R2 refers to Responder's second bid, etc.

| O2 | R2 | Meaning | Expected O3 |
|---|---|---|---|
| 2♦ | Pass | four+ ♦s 0-10 HCP, may have Major | pass |
|  | 2♥ | 5♥/4♠ weak | pass |
|  | 2♠ | 5♠/4♥ weak | pass |
|  | 2NT | 11-12HCP a major 4 | 14HCP 3NT or pass |
|  | 3♣ | Weak 6 card suit | pass |
|  | 3♥ | 5 hearts 13-17 HCPs Game Force | 3NT or 4♥ |
|  | 3♠ | 5 spades 13-17 HCPs Game Force | 3NT or 4♠ |
|  | 3NT | 13-17HCP and a major 4 | pass |
|  | 4♥ | 5/5 in majors with 13-16 points | Pass or 4♠ |
| 2♥ | Pass | Weak at least 4♥ | pass |
|  | 2NT | 11-12 HCP four ♠ less than four ♥ | 14p 3NT or pass |
|  | 3♣/♦ | Weak 6 card suit | pass |
|  | 3♥ | 11-12 HCP four ♥ | 14p 4♥ or pass |
|  | 3♠ | 5 spades 13-17 HCPs Game Force | 3NT or 4♠ |
|  | 3NT | 13-17 HCP four ♠ less than four ♥ | Pass or 14p and four ♠, 4♠ |
|  | 4♥ | 13 points four ♥ | pass |
| 2♠ | Pass | At least 4 spades weak | pass |
|  | 2NT | 11-12 HCP four ♥ less than four ♠ | 14p 3NT or pass |
|  | 3♣/♦ | weak 6 card suit | pass |
|  | 3♥ | 5 hearts 13-17 HCPs Game Force | 3NT or 4♥ |
|  | 3♠ | 11-12 HCP four ♠ | 14p 4♠ or pass |
|  | 3NT | 13-17 HCP four ♥ less than four ♠ | Pass |
|  | 4♠ | 13 points four ♠ | Pass |

**Table 5  Stayman & Transfers over suit interference.**
General principle: X indicates that was my bid and suit normal transfer.

| Opener | Overcall | Responder | Meaning |
|---|---|---|---|
| 1NT | 2♣ | X | Stayman |
|  |  | 2♦/♥ | Normal transfer |
|  |  | 2♠/NT | normal + stop in indicated suit |
|  | 2♦ | X | transfer to ♥ |
|  |  | 2♥ | transfer to ♠ |
|  |  | 2♠/NT | normal + stop in indicated suit |
|  | 2♥ | X | transfer to ♠ |
|  |  | 2♠/NT | normal + stop in indicated suit |
|  | 2♠ | X | 11 HCPs and stop in spades |
|  |  | 2NT | 12 HCPs and stop in spades |
|  |  |  |  |

**Table 6 Wriggle: Transfer over 1NT doubled, for all cases.**
If the opponents bid, revert to natural, in general don't bid. Table assumes opponents double 1NT then remain silent. Note responder cannot have more than 13HCP

| Open1 | Over-caller | Responder 1 | open2 | Responder 2 |
|---|---|---|---|---|
| 1NT | X | XX 0-8 HCP | 2♣ | With a very unbalanced |
|  |  | 2♣ 0-8 HCP | 2♦ | hand and a long suit |
|  |  | 2♦ 0-8 HCP | 2♥ | can raise to appropriate |
|  |  | 2♥ 0-8 HCP | 2♠ | level. |
|  |  | 2♠ not used |  |  |
|  |  | Pass no 5 card suit, FORCE: 1 round 0-12 HCP | XX | pass for penalties 9+HCP, or bid 4 card suits up line 0-8 HCP |
|  |  | 2NT not used |  |  |
|  |  | 3NT 13 HCP Balanced | Pass | * When Opener is vulnerable and opponents not, 3NT makes 600 versus 1NT X -3 makes 500 |

## Table 7 Wriggle For sequence 1NT P P X P P ..

requires modified approach as pass by responder terminates bidding. We cannot apply transfers and responder has <11HCP & unlikely to have a five card suit. If the opponents bid NT or a suit pass gracefully (or did I mean gratefully).

| Responder's 2nd | Opener's 3$^{rd}$ bid | |
|---|---|---|
| Pass 9-10 HCP | | |
| XX 0-8 HCP | Bid up the line | |
| suit | natural | |
| | | |

Contents

# Appendix D

## Wigan ¾ Howell Movement Cards 4 Tables

| Table 1 | | | | Table 2 | | | |
|---|---|---|---|---|---|---|---|
| Rd | NS | EW | Boards | Rd | NS | EW | Boards |
| 1 | 1 | 2 | 1- 4 | 1 | 3 | 4 | 5- 8 |
| 2 | 2 | 5 | 13-16 | 2 | 3 | 1 | 21-24 |
| 3 | 5 | 8 | 17-20 | 3 | 3 | 2 | 9-12 |
| 4 | 3 | 6 | 5- 8 | 4 | 3 | 5 | 1- 4 |
| 5 | 6 | 4 | 21-24 | 5 | 3 | 8 | 13-16 |
| 6 | 4 | 1 | 9-12 | 6 | 3 | 6 | 17-20 |
| Table 3 | | | | Table 4 | | | |
| Rd | NS | EW | Boards | Rd | NS | EW | Boards |
| 1 | 5 | 6 | 9-12 | 1 | 7 | 8 | 9-12 |
| 2 | 4 | 8 | 1- 4 | 2 | 6 | 7 | 1- 4 |
| 3 | 6 | 1 | 13-16 | 3 | 7 | 4 | 13-16 |
| 4 | 2 | 4 | 17-20 | 4 | 1 | 7 | 17-20 |
| 5 | 1 | 5 | 5- 8 | 5 | 7 | 2 | 5- 8 |
| 6 | 8 | 2 | 21-24 | 6 | 5 | 7 | 21-24 |

Contents

# Appendix E
# Bidding (System) Card

| | Name Bev Pardoe | EBU No. |
|---|---|---|
| | Partner | EBU No. |

| General Description of Bidding Methods |
|---|
| Bev's Benji-Acol |

| 1NT Openings and Responses ||||
|---|---|---|---|
| Strength | 12 – 14 HCPs | Tick if artificial and provided detail below ☐ ||
| Shape Constraints | no 5 card major | Tick if may have singleton ☐ ||
| Responses | | 2♣ Stayman: non-promissory ||
| 2♦ | Transfer to ♥s | 2♥ | Transfer to ♠ |
| 2♠ | 11 HCPs balanced | 2NT | 12 HCPs balanced |
| | Others 3♣/♦/♥/♠ = 5+ card suit and slam interest |||
| Action after opponents double || Systems On, Wriggle ||
| Action after other interference || System On where possible ||

| Two-Level Openings and Responses |||
|---|---|---|
| | Meaning | Responses |
| 2♣ | 8 maj./9min. pts no point count | 2♦ negative |
| 2♦ | 23+ balanced 20+ 5:4 suits | 2♥ -ve, 2♠ +ve, 2NT weak bal. |
| 2♥ | Weak 6-9 HCPs 6 cards | 2♠ Ogust |
| 2♠ | Weak 6-9 HCPs 6 cards | 2NT Ogust |
| 2NT | 20-22 HCPs balanced | 3♣ Stayman and transfers |

| Notes |
|---|
| Bid 4 card suits up the line |

## Other Opening Bids

|  | HCP | See note | Min Length | Conventional meaning | Special Responses |
|---|---|---|---|---|---|
| 1♣ | 10-19 | ☐ | 4 | HCPs + length >= to 20 | 1NT 6-9 HCPs |
| 1♦ | 10-19 | ☐ | 4 | | 2NT 10-12 |
| 1♥ | 10-19 | ☐ | 4 | | Limit raises see note 3 |
| 1♠ | 10-19 | ☐ | 4 | | |
| 3 bids | 6-10 | ☐ | 7 | Pre-emptive | 7 losers NV 6 V |
| 4 bids | 6-10 | ☐ | 8 | Pre-emptive | 6 losers NV 5 V |

NV means non-vulnerable and V means vulnerable

## Defensive Methods after Opponents Open

| Opponents open a natural one of a suit | Conventional meaning | Special responses |
|---|---|---|
| 1 Level overcall | 8 to 11 HCPs SQ 7 | |
| 2 Level overcall | 12 to 15 HCPs SQ 8, ex. 2♣ 8-15 HCPs SQ >= 7 | |
| 3 level overcall | 7 card suit 6 to 9 HCPs | |
| Jump overcall | Intermediate 12-16, good 6-card suit | |
| Michaels Cue bid | Two highest unbid suit 5:5  10 HCPs | |
| 1NT     Direct: Protective: | 15-17 12-14 note 4 | As for 1NT opening |
| 2NT Unusual | 2 lowest unbid suits 5:5 10 HCPs | |

| OPPONENTS OPEN WITH | DEFENSIVE METHODS |
|---|---|
| Strong 1♣ | Natural |
| Short 1♣/1♦ | Natural |
| Strong 1NT | Double = penalties; 2♣ /♦ Astro 13+ HCPs 2♥ /♠ Nat |
| Weak 2 | See note 1 |
| Weak 3 | Double = take out, suit natural |
| 4 bids | Double = take out |
| Michael's | See note 6 |
| Multi 2♦ | See note 2 |

## Slam Conventions

| Name | Meaning of response |
|---|---|
| 4♣ Gerber | 4♦ 0 or 4 Aces 4♥ 1, 4♠ 2 and 4NT 3 |
| 4NT RKCB | 5♣ 0or3 , 5♦ 1or3 ,5♥ 2 no Q, 5♠ 2 + Q |

### COMPETITIVE AUCTIONS

Agreements after opening of one of a suit and overcall by opponents Level to which negative doubles apply 2♠

Agreements after opponents double for take-out

| Redouble 9+ HCP | New suit 10-11 HCPs | Jump in new suit 12+ HCPs |
|---|---|---|

With 4 cards in bid suit X: stretch raises; 2NT = raise to 3, raise to 2 on 0 – 5, & raise to 3 with 6-9

### OTHER CONVENTIONS

**Fourth Suit Forcing**: A bid in the fourth suit is artificial, showing no particular holding in that suit but requesting partner to describe his/her hand further.

After 1♣ - 1♦ - 1♥, 1♠ is natural and 2♠ is 'fourth suit forcing'.

At the 3 Level is often asking for a stop for NT

**Splinter**, double jump after opening bid

**Cue Bids** new suit at 4 Level after suit agreement.

**After suit agreement** new suit is asking.

### SUPPLEMENTARY DETAILS

1. 2 level overcall is normal with a weaker suit. 2NT and lower 3 Level overcalls are two suiters

2. 2nd seat 2 Level overcalls are normal, 2NT Unusual and 3 level 6 card suit X for take out. 4th set X : my bid 2 Level overcall normal, 2NT Unusual and 3 Level bids 6 card suit all with opening points

3 **NT rebids**: After 1 level response 1NT = 15-16; 2NT = 17-18; 3NT = 19

4 **Protective 1NT overcall**: After an opening bid and 2 passes, 1NT shows 12-15.
   With more points, double first and rebid NT over partner's response.

## Opening Leads

| | | | | | | | |
|---|---|---|---|---|---|---|---|
| v. suit contracts | A **K** | **A** K x | **K** Q 10 | **K** Q x | K **J** 10 | K **10** 9 |
| | **Q** J x | **J** 10 x | 10 x **x** | **10** 9 x | 9 **8** 7 x | 10 x x **x** |
| | H x x **x** | H x x **x** x | H x x **x** x x | **x** x | x **x** x | x **x** x x |
| v. NT contracts | **A** K x (**x**) | A **J** 10 x | **K** Q 10 | **K** Q x | K **J** 10 | K **10** 9 |
| | **Q** J x | **J** 10 x | 10 x **x** | **10** 9 x | 9 **8** 7 x | 10 x x **x** |
| | H x x **x** | H x x **x** x | H x x **x** x x | **x** x | x **x** x | x **x** x x |

## Carding Methods

| | Primary method v suit contracts | Primary method v NT contracts |
|---|---|---|
| On Partner's lead | McKinney | High encouraging |
| On Declarer's lead | McKinney | McKinney |
| When discarding | McKinney | McKinney |

## SUPPLEMENTARY DETAILS (continued)

5. Defence against Jugglers Club: to open and in 2$^{nd}$ seat over bid hand to obstruct their bidding. X of weak NT on one point more than their max.

6. Defence against Michael's, with 4+ cards in suit, 2NT = 10-12 points, 3 suit = 6-9 points and X = 0-5 points

Contents

# Appendix F

## Glossary of Bridge terms

**Advancer**: 3rd caller after and opening bid, Overcaller's partner
**bid**: any call from: a suit or NT, bids are a subset of calls
**boundaries**: The upper and lower limits of points required for a specific level of play.
**call**: any call from: Pass, a suit, an NT, double,X or redouble,XX
**deal**: a pack distributed in fours hand of 13 cards
**dealer**: notional dealer, first player to call
**Director**, person in charge of the session who also acts as referee
**double**, X: may be asking partner to bid, for penalties or -ve showing a wish to bid
**finesse**: to play towards a tenace and play lower card in the hope RHO has the higher card.
**Forcing**: your partner makes a bid, and with no intervening bid from the opposition, you must bid.
**HCP**: high card points A=4, K=3, Q=2 & J=1
**L**: length points 5 card suit = 1, 6 card suit = 2 etc
**LHO**: left hand opponent
**hand**: 13 cards dealt from a pack of 52
**Opener**: first player to bid.
**Overcaller**: Opener's left hand opponent, LHO
**pack**: 52 cards in four suit, 2 to A in each
**points**: sum of HCP and length or shortage points
**quantification**: defining you hand by points or HCP
**rag**: any card less than a ten
**redouble**, XX: may be for penalties or asking partner to bid
**Responder**: opening bidder's partner
**RHO**: right hand opponent
**S**: shortage points, after finding a fit void=5, singleton=3, doubleton =1
**sacrifice**: bidding a contract you expect to fail that should lose less points than the contract bid by your opponents would make.
**stiff:** specified cards with no others, e.g. AK stiff
**stop card**: a bidding card that alerts your partner and the opposition that

you passed over a lower bid that was available to you. e.g. bidding 3♦s when you could have bid 2♦s.

**tenaces**: a combination of cards such as AQxx used for a finesse.

Contents

Printed in Great Britain
by Amazon